COUNTRY CRAFTS

COUNTRY CRAFTS

KITCHEN • PANTRY • DECORATION • STYLE

STEPHANIE DONALDSON

PHOTOGRAPHS BY MICHELLE GARRETT

To Ann — a consistently creative cook and valued friend

This edition is published by Aquamarine,
an imprint of Anness Publishing Ltd,
Blaby Road, Wigston, Leicestershire LE18 4SE;
info@anness.com

www.aquamarinebooks.com; www.annesspublishing.com

If you like the images in this book and would like to investigate using them for publishing, promotions or advertising, please visit our website www.practicalpictures.com for more information.

Publisher: Joanna Lorenz
Editorial Manager: Helen Sudell
Designer: Lisa Tai
Photographer: Michelle Garrett

Picture credits: Bridgeman Art Library, London:
p12 *Preparing for Dinner* by Frederick Daniel Hardy, Wolverhampton Art Gallery; p13 *Preserving Jam* by Frederick Daniel Hardy, Bourne Gallery, Reigate.

NOTES

Bracketed terms are intended for American readers.

For all recipes, quantities are given in both metric and imperial measures and, where appropriate, in standard cups and spoons. Follow one set of measures, but not a mixture, because they are not interchangeable.

Standard spoon and cup measures are level. 1 tsp = 5ml, 1 tbsp = 15ml, 1 cup = 250ml/8fl oz.

Australian standard tablespoons are 20ml. Australian readers should use 3 tsp in place of 1 tbsp for measuring small quantities.

American pints are 16fl oz/2 cups. American readers should use 20fl oz/2.5 cups in place of 1 pint when measuring liquids.

Electric oven temperatures in this book are for conventional ovens. When using a fan oven, the temperature will probably need to be reduced by about 10-20°C/20-40°F. Since ovens vary, you should check with your manufacturer's instruction book for guidance.

Medium (US large) eggs are used unless otherwise stated.

PUBLISHER'S NOTE

Although the advice and information in this book are believed to be accurate and true at the time of going to press, neither the authors nor the publisher can accept any legal responsibility or liability for any errors or omissions that may have been made nor for any inaccuracies nor for any loss, harm or injury that comes about from following instructions or advice in this book.

Sections of this book contain information on herbs and essential oils and their uses, but this is not intended as a practical guide to self-medication. Neither the author nor the publisher can be held responsible for any specific individual's reactions, harmful effects or claims arising from the use of the general data and suggestions it contains, whether in recipe form or otherwise. Many plants are poisonous, all can be toxic if used inappropriately, and the advice of a qualified medical practitioner should always be sought before using any herbal treatments or remedies, especially if you are pregnant. The use of any information contained in this book is entirely at the reader's sole discretion and risk.

Some of the projects in this book use candles. Take care at all times to ensure that candles are firmly secured and that lighted candles are never left unattended. An effective flame-resistant spray can be applied to displays, though this will not make them fireproof.

Contents

Introduction 6

The Pantry 22

The Bathroom 74

The Still Room 98

Seasonal Celebrations 124

Seasonal Checklist 146

Useful Sources and Suppliers 156

Index 158

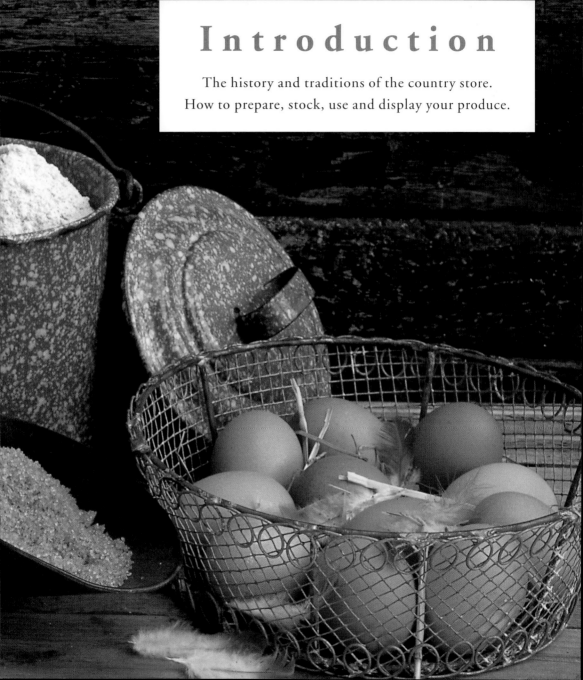

Introduction

The history and traditions of the country store.
How to prepare, stock, use and display your produce.

A simpler way of life

Our constant search for progress has resulted in a world where, for many of us, the seasons have become largely irrelevant, except as a backdrop for a change of clothing and sporting activities. We can eat fresh cherries from Chile in winter, avocados from Israel throughout the year, and, like children, indulge our every culinary whim regardless of the time or season of the year.

The price we pay for this is not just the financial and environmental cost of these unseasonal foods, but it is also an alienation from our instincts to sow, grow, reap and store, to mark the change of the seasons in festivals and thanksgiving and to pass on the knowledge of how to do these things to future generations.

There is still a hunger in us for these old ways, and although few of us regret the advent of many of modern life's labour-saving devices and comforts, we are drawn to the simplicity of earlier times when survival was a reward rather than an expectation. Although we no longer need to follow the progress of the seasons to ensure our survival, we can still participate in seasonal activities and will find our lives greatly enriched by doing so.

The sowing of seeds, even if it is a pot of parsley on the windowsill, is the beginning of a relationship with plants that germinate, picking apples from the garden follows the beauty of the spring blossom and the slow growth of the tiny green fruit to full-flushed maturity when we can enjoy the satisfaction of our own harvest.

I hope very much that this book will inspire you to take some time out of our busy and hectic modern life to experience for yourself the pleasure of the seasons: to discover the enjoyment to be had in baking, pickling and preserving; to try the simple natural remedies and fragrant beauty products and potpourris; and to celebrate the progress of the year with seasonal decorations and foods.

Right: *An assortment of invaluable items to collect for your still room: blocks of beeswax, candles, flower waters, essential oils, dried herbs and flowerheads.*

The history of the store cupboard

I n the Middle Ages, the monasteries were the repositories of knowledge, and high ranking among the monks was the cellarer who had overall responsibility for providing the religious community with all the food and drink that was needed throughout the year. He was an expert in the growing, harvesting and preserving of large quantities of food, and while life in general was short and not very sweet, the religious orders were well nourished and far healthier than the general populace. The cellarer's knowledge of herbs and spices, of salts, vinegars and oils increased as new plants and flavourings were introduced from other lands, and his uses of them, as well as his observations, were meticulously recorded in what were the forebears of our modern recipe books.

In Elizabethan England it became customary for gentlewomen to write down the secrets of their household management in a book to pass on their skills from one generation to the next. As well as recipes, this book would include simple remedies, lotions and potions, potpourris and polishes, many of which we would recognize and even keep in our pantry today.

As the ability to read and write spread among the population, this tradition was taken up more generally, and for generations people passed on and exchanged recipes with friends and family to keep the store cupboard full. It was not until Victorian times, and the advent of tomes such as Mrs Beeton's *Book of Household Management*, that this knowledge passed from the family into the hands of 'experts' and began to acquire a mystique that removed it from its common part of our everyday lives.

Above: *In the past, salt was of great social and economic importance and was an extremely valuable commodity.*

Left: *In former times, all but the poorest households would have owned a cow and the dairy was as important as the still room to the countrywoman.*

Right: *Blue and white enamelware is enduringly popular, and is appreciated today as much as ever for its durability, practicality and simple design.*

Traditions, folklore and fact

In the days when good husbandry was an essential skill for every country dweller, the circle of the seasons entailed an endless progression of tasks that had to be completed to ensure the fertility and productivity of the land followed by a fruitful harvest that would see the family through the long winter.

Everyone had their tasks: even the smallest of the children would be put to work picking stones, scaring the birds and gathering fruit and vegetables. As the daughters grew up they would learn the skills of the kitchen, the dairy and still room from their mother, and by the time they left to make their own homes, they would be accomplished in all the necessary tasks of everyday life. For everyone, such important festivals as Easter, Harvest Festival, Thanksgiving and Christmas were markers in the year, and these family celebrations were rewards for the hard work of daily life as well as religious occasions.

Many folk tales and traditional rhymes were originally devised as a reminder of the seasonal tasks. In Tudor England, for example, the poet and writer Thomas Tusser

Below: Preparing food for the table was a lengthy task. Vegetables would have to be picked from the garden, scrubbed clean and then peeled before being chopped up for the pot.

was particularly free with his advice, instructing farmer and housewife alike in books with edifying titles such as *Five Hundred Points of Good Husbandry* and *Housewifely Admonitions*. A typical example of his rhyming recommendations is this little verse on the efficacy of wormwood to prevent the infestation of houses by fleas:

While wormwood hath seed, get a bundle or twain,
to save against March, to make flea to refrain:
Where chamber is sweept, and wormwood is strown,
no flea, for his life, dare abide to be known.

In other words, wormwood should be picked when it has set seed in the late summer or autumn, hung up to dry over winter and then used at the time of spring cleaning in early spring, when it will be most effective against fleas. In an age when books were a luxury, such rhymes made it easier to remember advice and knowledge.

Above: *Making jams, jellies and preserves would have been an activity that the whole family played a part in, from collecting fruits from the hedgerows around the house or farm to helping mother with the cooking – and eating – of the produce.*

Although superstition and folklore certainly played their part in rural life, country people have always been, by and large, great realists and were far too busy working to spend much time on spells and potions. These were mainly the province of doctors and charlatans, whose cures were frequently more dangerous than the illness itself. Country people preferred to rely on simple remedies, which every housewife prepared in her still room. Just as we once again appreciate the quality of home-made preserves and provender, so we are also acknowledging that many of the old natural remedies were based on understanding rather than superstition, and have some merit when it comes to treating minor ailments.

13

Preparing your store

It is quite possible to make practically everything shown and described in this book without having to buy any special equipment, but the projects will be easier to do if you have a good range of basic kitchen equipment. The following items are recommended.

- a large, heavy pan for preserving and sterilizing
- a good selection of clean glass jars and bottles
- fresh rubber seals for preserving jars
- accurate scales
- measuring jugs and cups
- a selection of mixing bowls
- a *bain-marie* or double boiler – if you are also going to make cosmetics, you will need a second bowl to fit your pan, which you should keep purely for this purpose. Also keep a set of the following utensils for making cosmetics only:
- metal whisk
- wooden spoon
- set of measuring spoons

BASIC MATERIALS AND INGREDIENTS

If you are fortunate enough to live in the country, you may already have a productive garden and access to fruitful hedgerows and woodlands to provide many of the basic materials from which you can begin to fill your country store, but for those of us less blessed, there is still the pleasure of making, even if we do not do the growing and the gathering ourselves. The best farm stores are a good source of freshly picked fruit and vegetables, as are the farms where you can pick your own produce. Even city dwellers will find many bargains at their local market, especially at the end of the day when a whole box can be bought at a knock-down price. An elderly neighbour whose garden is becoming neglected may welcome your planting a vegetable patch and sharing the produce with them. And in a fruitful year, a friend with an apple tree will consider you are doing them a favour if you ask for some fruit.

Everyone should grow some herbs. They give our food savour, stimulate the appetite, are health-giving and a fragrant addition to the home. Herbs are widely used in the projects in this book, and whatever the scale of your herb garden, whether a windowsill or a formal garden, you will be able to make use of everything you grow.

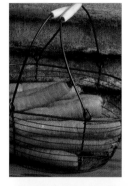

Left: *Use a wire basket for picking produce; excess soil can drop through the base and good air circulation keeps the vegetables in prime condition for several days.*

Below: *Fresh ingredients, whether home-grown or bought, are the starting point and the inspiration for nearly everything you will make for your store cupboard or pantry.*

Above: *There is an intrinsic beauty to old, well-used kitchen utensils and equipment, and provided they do the job and can be properly cleaned, there is no need to replace them with more modern equivalents.*

Right: *Cox's Orange Pippin apples may not have the glossy perfection of some other varieties found in stores and markets, but their flavour is unsurpassed.*

Whether you are collecting ingredients for cooking, for natural remedies, for fragrance or celebration, it is vitally important that they are always of the highest possible quality. For example, for bottling, fully ripe but firm fruit will give the best flavour. Herbs are at their most potent just before they flower. Vegetables should be used as soon as possible after they have been picked or bought. Essential oils should always be purchased from a reputable supplier, and dried flowers should be from the most recent harvest. In other words, quite simply, if your intention is to make a quality product, you must use only quality ingredients.

Growing and gathering for your store

One of the great advantages of growing your own produce is that you know precisely what has been used on the plants: no over-enthusiastic applications of fertilizers or other chemicals. Ideally, just the sweat of your brow and lots of compost. If possible grow your vegetables, fruit and herbs organically because they will be better for you and organic cultivation is also better for the health of the soil. If you do need to control pests, try to use natural predators wherever possible. They are increasingly available and as effective as chemical sprays when used correctly.

BUYING FOR YOUR STORE
Organically grown foods are also available from specialist food stores and some supermarkets. While they do not always have the perfection of their chemically stimulated relatives, their flavour is generally excellent. Remember that what you wish to preserve is flavour and fragrance, so it is important to choose varieties that have these attributes; a visually perfect red apple that has the texture of cotton wool will not taste any better once it has been bottled.

GATHERING FOR YOUR STORE
Fortunately, it is now a little easier to collect fruits, berries and nuts from the hedgerows as the days when farmers and highway maintenance teams sprayed our roadsides with weedkillers are mostly past. There is a welcome return of a profusion of wild flowers that make verges and field margins so lovely in the spring and summer months and a corresponding burgeoning of hedgerows with abundant elderflowers, blackberries, sloes, hips and haws. When gathering from the wild, always do so respectfully. Always make sure that you leave plenty for the wildlife, as the hedgerow is an important food source for them, and also something for others who would like to share in the bounty. Never pick an endangered species. It is your responsibility to find out which plants are protected in your area and it is important that you do so; your local council or library will be able to help you.

Anyone who has gathered blackberries, sloes or wild strawberries will tell you that it takes a surprisingly long time to collect a usable quantity, and it always seems that the best and most plenteous fruit is just out of reach. So make gathering a group activity, preferably with people of varying heights and including someone with a hooked stick to reach those elusive branches. What can be a chore for an individual can be fun for the whole family, who will also benefit from the fresh air and exercise.

Right: *Home-grown peas have an unrivalled flavour and shelling them while sitting in the sunshine is a restful occupation.*

Above: *Sow small quantities of seeds frequently in order to provide a succession of produce throughout the season.*

Above: *Beetroot (beet) thinnings provide delicious baby beets and the leaves can be cooked just like spinach.*

Right: *Gather your herbs in the morning when they are at their most aromatic and pick them regularly as this will ensure that they are at their freshest.*

HARVESTING FOR YOUR STORE

This is the time when your efforts are rewarded, when those carefully nurtured fruits, vegetables, blossoms and herbs are gathered in ready to be used to fill your store. Choose your harvest time carefully; a dry sunny day with a light breeze is ideal – for you and the produce. Flowers and herbs should be gathered only after the dew has dried but before midday. You must pick fruit carefully to avoid bruising or damaging them in any way. Young vegetables should be gathered in small batches for immediate use and mature root vegetables lifted before the first frosts.

17

Using and displaying
your store cupboard

There is a temptation to treat the contents of the store cupboard or pantry rather like works of art, treasures to be displayed and admired but never touched, but this is to miss out on the best bit of all – the consumption. Once you have tasted and enjoyed the fruits of your labours, it becomes easier to accept that your store is an ever-changing Aladdin's cave of treats rather than an end in itself.

If considerations of space, time and money permit it, then a cool, dark larder or cellar is the perfect place to keep jams, jellies, pickles and preserves, but failing that, set aside a cupboard in your kitchen for storing home-made produce. Warm, light rooms are not ideal for the storage of preserves or for drying flowers and herbs, but if you dry some flowers and herbs especially for display and have a shelf where you can show off your preserves for a short period before use, then you can keep the majority of your produce in good condition while not missing out on the compliments.

Above: *Miniature galvanized buckets can be used as attractive containers for a collection of medicinal herbs and flowers.*

Left: *Turn your fresh herbs into an attractive feature in a room by storing them in pretty glass containers.*

Right: *Autumn leaves and bows made out of raffia or coarse string can give your jars of preserves an attractive rustic finish.*

Decorating and presenting

The finishing touches can turn an everyday item into something special. A simple pot of preserves, for instance, becomes a special gift when it is presented in a pretty jar with the lid covered by a beautiful autumn leaf tied on with raffia. And a bottle of aromatic chilli oil does not need a written label to identify its flavourings when its neck is decorated with a bunch of chillies.

Colourful sweetmeats are all the more tempting for being individually packaged in cellophane and tied with a raffia bow, or nestling inside a decorative wooden box.

Celebration wines and ratafias become sublime when bottled in decorative glass bottles and adorned with gilded leaves and corks.

Above: *A decorative touch turns this lemon- and lime-flavoured vinegar into a perfect gift.*

Above: *Natural materials make inexpensive and very attractive packaging.*

Left: *A dried orange slice tied around a jar of marmalade is an unusual but eloquent label.*

Right: *The autumnal colours of the potpourri are echoed in the matt-brown ribbon and the sisal string used to decorate the cellophane bag.*

The Pantry

An irresistible collection of preserves, flavoured oils
and vinegars, baked goods and sweet gifts.

Fruit and vegetables

Whether the fruit and vegetables you use are from your garden or from elsewhere, produce that is destined for preserving should always be of the best possible quality. When growing your own produce, choose the varieties whose good flavour is particularly mentioned. It is amazing how many modern varieties that are grown for disease resistance and reliability seem to have sacrificed flavour in the search for the standardization of colour and size. Therefore, if you are buying fruit and vegetables, it is always a good idea to taste them before you start preserving, just to make sure that they have a flavour that is worth keeping. Less than perfect fruit such as windfalls can be used to make jellies, but because they deteriorate quickly, you should be ready for action as soon as you have collected them.

Wherever possible, store your fruit and vegetables in a dark, cool but frost-free place with good ventilation. They will keep extremely well in these conditions, especially if they are prepared for storage beforehand. Mature root vegetables such as carrots, parsnips and beetroots (beets) will keep for months when stored in boxes of sand (it must be horticultural, not builder's, sand). Apples and pears can be kept on slatted wooden shelves, if they are not touching, or you can individually wrap them in paper and store them in boxes. They should last through the winter, especially if the varieties stored are good keepers such as Russet apples and Conference pears.

You must never store fruit near potatoes because it will become tainted. It is important to check your stored fruit and vegetables regularly, using the fruit as it ripens and removing any that shows signs of rot or this will spread through the good fruit.

Below: *The flavour of tomatoes is improved by storing them at room temperature rather than in a refrigerator. Ideally, tomatoes should not be picked until they are fully ripe, but even an under-ripe fruit will improve if you store it in this way.*

Above: *At harvest time, prepare unblemished apples for storage. Each fruit should be carefully wrapped in newspaper and stored on a wooden tray or in a cardboard box. Alternatively, store them unwrapped and not touching on slatted, wooden shelves.*

Right: *The traditional way of storing mature root vegetables is to arrange them in layers in silver sand. Then cover them completely and store in a cool, dark place and they will keep for months, retaining a good flavour and texture.*

Herbs and flowers

If you have enough space in your garden, devoting a corner to the growing of herbs and flowers for drying will save you a great deal of money.

Herbs vary enormously in their aromatic strength and it is worth the time and expense to find a reputable herb grower who can sell you recommended named varieties of the herbs. If you do not have space to grow all the herbs you will need, there are companies that sell good-quality fresh and dried herbs by mail order far more cheaply than you can buy them at a supermarket. It is also worthwhile visiting stores that cater for Indian and South-east Asian communities as a source of high-quality herbs and spices.

Herbs should be harvested before they have flowered, on a dry morning when the volatile oils will be at their most concentrated. From noon onwards the oils start to evaporate into the air and flavour and fragrance are diminished.

Although herbs look very decorative when hung in open bunches from an old-fashioned clothes-airer, this is not the best way to dry them. Rather, the bunches of herbs should be rolled up in cones of brown paper, which will protect them from the light, then hung up to dry. Once they are fully dry (usually about two weeks), they should be taken down, stripped from their stems and stored in coloured glass bottles away from the light. This will ensure that when you come to use the herbs for cooking or fragrance, they will still be intensely aromatic.

When growing flowers specifically for drying, it is worth concentrating on the varieties that are difficult to come by or expensive, such as peonies and roses. Unless you have limitless space, there is little point in growing huge quantities of statice and helichrysum as these can be bought fairly easily and inexpensively.

When picking flowers for drying, they should be in full bloom but not full blown or they will drop their petals. They are also best gathered in the morning of a dry day. Hang them upside down in bunches in a warm, preferably not too light position and leave them there until they are dry to the touch. Peonies need to be dry right into the

Left and Above: *A simple but very effective method of preserving your fresh herbs is to place them in a jar with a tight-fitting lid that contains sea salt. The herbs will then remain just as fresh and full of flavour as the day they were picked, and they will also give a delicious and distinctive flavour to the salt.*

Above: *Fresh herbs should be picked early in the day, once the dew has dried, to capture the full intensity of their flavour. Keep them cool indoors until you are ready to use them, and replace them as soon as they start to look rather limp and bedraggled.*

Left: *The best way to dry fresh flowers is to tie them loosely in small bundles and hang them upside-down in a well-ventilated room. Keep them out of direct sunlight to retain their vibrant colours.*

centre of the flower and, to achieve this, it is advisable to place them in a low oven for about four hours after they have air-dried. Once you are confident that your flowers are fully dry, pack them into boxes and store in a dry place until you wish to use them. It is important to store dried flowers in boxes in order to keep them free of dust and preserve their colour.

When buying dried flowers, it is best to purchase them from the grower, as these will have been stored in the best possible conditions and will not have been handled many times, which often happens to dried flowers before they reach your local store. Bargain dried flowers are nearly always old stock from the harvest before last and are not worth buying as they are brittle and faded.

Preserving produce

Preserving and drying are time-honoured methods for prolonging the life of fruit, vegetables, herbs and sometimes flowers.

PRESERVING
Food can be preserved by being bottled in a variety of natural preservatives. Vegetables and herbs may be preserved by being packed in salt or immersed in brine. They can also be kept in oil, or used in small amounts to flavour oil.

Vegetables, fruit and herbs can be pickled in or used to flavour vinegar and lemon juice. Even sugar and honey can be used for preserving fruit, herbs and flowers or can be flavoured by them. Fruit, herbs and flowers can also be preserved in alcohol or turned into wines and liqueurs.

DRYING
Vegetables, herbs, fruit and flowers can all be preserved by being air-dried or placed in an oven set at a low temperature.

STERILIZING JARS IN WATER

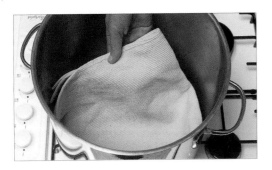

1 *Line the base of the sterilizing pan with either a folded cloth or a wooden trivet.*

2 *Place the bottles in the pan and fold cloths around each one to prevent them touching.*

3 *Fill the pan with cold water so that the bottles are covered by at least 2.5cm/1in of water.*

4 *Once the bottles have cooled, check the seals by loosening the clips and making sure that they stay intact.*

STERILIZING

To ensure that harmful bacteria are eliminated from fruit and vegetables bottled in brine, syrup or their own juices, it is necessary to sterilize the bottles in a water bath or in the oven. To sterilize in water, follow the step instructions on the facing page. Alternatively, rest the lids on the bottles but do not seal. Stand them on a baking sheet lined with newspaper and place in a low oven, 120°C/250°F/Gas ½.

Above: *Whether dried, bottled in syrup or preserved in oil, there is a surprising beauty to many home-made preserves.*

Remove and seal immediately. As the bottles cool, a vacuum forms inside to complete the seal. Always use clean, undamaged bottles with fresh seals, and test every seal by turning it upside down. Bottles with failed seals should be used immediately.

Choosing and preparing containers

Glass jars and bottles have been used for the majority of projects in this chapter. Glass is durable, versatile and decorative. Its advantage over metal, earthenware, terracotta and porcelain is that it reveals and enhances its contents. Modern recycled glass has many of the qualities of antique glass such as flaws and colourings, and is inexpensive. Old-fashioned sweet (candy) jars, preserving jars and preserve pots can still be bought in junk stores and, providing that they can be properly cleaned, used to great effect. They must not be used for any bottling that requires sterilizing.

STERILIZING JARS
To sterilize jars in a dishwasher, use the hottest wash without any detergent. However, if you do not own a dishwasher, you can sterilize in the following way. First, wash the jars in hot, soapy water and rinse thoroughly. Stand them the right way up on a wooden board (making sure that they are not touching) and place the board in a cold oven. Turn the oven to very low (110°C/225°F/Gas ¼) and leave the jars for 30 minutes. If they are not to be used immediately, cover with a clean cloth.

Above: *Old-fashioned glass bottles are full of character and very attractive. They may be used for projects where containers should be clean but not necessarily sterile.*

Above: *There is a variety of bottles and jars that are designed for preserving, and provided they are not damaged in any way, they can be reused. However, you should always use fresh seals.*

SEALS

The type and effectiveness of the seal required depend on the process used. Providing jam (jelly) jars are thoroughly washed and dried before use, a circle of baking parchment and a paper cover are sufficient to keep the contents in good condition. Wines and liqueurs keep well in bottles sealed with new corks. Vinegars and oils can be sealed with either corks or screw tops, but bottled fruit and vegetables must be sealed with new rubber seals.

Ideally, all your preserves should be labelled with a description of the contents and the date they were made. Self-adhesive labels may be attached to the surface of the

Above: With glass containers a descriptive label is not always necessary, but it is a good idea to record the date the preserve was made so that you use the contents of your store cupboard in rotation.

bottle or jar or, alternatively, attractive cardboard, wooden or metal labels may be tied round the neck. Bear in mind that if you intend to store your preserves in a cellar or larder (pantry) where conditions may be slightly damp and paper labels are liable to fall off or quickly deteriorate, it would be advisable to use something more durable, such as metal or wooden labels.

Flavoured oils

A selection of flavoured oils will bring the taste of high summer to your cooking all year round. All flavoured oils are best used within three months.

GARLIC OIL

Use this delicious oil in dressings and to brush on fish, meat and vegetables. In addition it saves the fiddly task of cleaning the garlic press every time you flavour with garlic! Do not throw away the poached garlic cloves that are removed from the oil before bottling: they are ambrosial when spread on fresh French bread or used as a relish on meat, fish or vegetables. Either use immediately or pack them into a glass jar, cover with oil and store in a refrigerator to use within ten days.

Makes 750ml/1¼ pints/3 cups
25 large plump garlic cloves
900ml/1½ pints/3¾ cups cold-pressed
  virgin olive oil

Above: Flavoured oils in glass bottles are attractive as well as useful ingredients.

1 Peel the garlic cloves.

2 Heat the oil to a gentle simmer in a small pan, then add the garlic cloves and poach them for about 25 minutes, until tender and translucent. Remove the pan from the heat and leave the mixture in the pan until cool.

3 Strain the garlic cloves from the oil, reserving them for another use. Pour the oil into a clean bottle, seal with a screw top or cork and use within ten days.

CHILLI OIL

In the south of France, pizzas are enlivened by drizzling chilli oil over them. You can also use this oil for stir-frying vegetables or grilling (broiling). For a more robust flavour, add garlic, thyme and peppercorns to this oil.

Makes 500ml/17fl oz/2¼ cups
500ml/17fl oz/2¼ cups virgin olive oil
1 small fresh green chilli
5 small fresh red chillies

Fill a clean, dry bottle with the olive oil. Slice the green chilli crossways into thin rings and add them with the whole red chillies to the oil.

Cork the bottle tightly with a new cork and leave the mixture to infuse for 10–14 days. Shake the bottle from time to time during this period.

SAFFRON OIL

Saffron has never been surpassed as a flavouring. By weight it is certainly among the most expensive of spices but a little saffron goes a long way, especially when you use it to infuse an oil with its delicate flavour and then brush the oil on to grilled (broiled) fish.

Makes 250ml/8fl oz/1 cup
a large pinch saffron strands
250ml/8fl oz/1 cup light olive oil or
  pure sunflower oil

Put the saffron strands in a clean dry bottle. Fill the bottle with oil and seal with a cork. Leave to infuse for two weeks, gently shaking the bottle daily, before using.

TERIYAKI MARINADE

This Japanese marinade is wonderful for barbecued and grilled meats. Marinate the meat for at least an hour before cooking.

Makes 375ml/13 fl oz/1½ cups

150ml/¼ pint/⅔ cup olive oil
150ml/¼ pint/⅔ cup soy sauce
30ml/2 tbsp grated fresh ginger
2 garlic cloves, crushed
15ml/1 tbsp grated
*   orange rind*
60ml/4 tbsp dry sherry

Above: *Flavoured oils are a good way of carrying the taste of the summer through into your winter cooking, as the freshness of the herbs and spices is captured in the oil.*

Place all of the ingredients into a wide-necked bottle or jar. Seal the container securely and then shake it vigorously until all the ingredients are thoroughly mixed. Leave the marinade overnight before using. It is best to store it in a cool place, out of direct sunlight.

WARNING: there is some evidence that oils containing fresh herbs and spices can grow harmful moulds, especially once the bottle has been opened and the contents are not fully covered by the oil. To protect against this, it is recommended that the herbs and spices are removed once their flavour has passed into the oil.

Flavoured vinegars

Fruit-flavoured vinegars give a delicious depth to salad dressings and, if used sparingly, will enhance the flavour of fruit such as strawberries and nectarines that are not quite ripe. All flavoured vinegars are best used within three months.

RASPBERRY VINEGAR
Makes 750ml/1¼ pints/3 cups, strained vinegar
600ml/1 pint/2½ cups red wine vinegar
15ml/1 tbsp pickling spice
450g/1lb/3 cups raspberries, fresh or frozen
2 sprigs fresh lemon thyme

Above: *Raspberry vinegar.*

1 *Pour the vinegar into a pan, add the spice and heat gently for five minutes.*

2 *Pour the hot vinegar mixture over the raspberries in a bowl and then add the lemon thyme. Cover and leave the mixture to infuse for two days in a cool, dark place, stirring occasionally.*

3 *Remove the thyme and raspberries and strain the liquid. Pour the flavoured vinegar into a clean, dry bottle and seal with a cork.*

LEMON AND LIME VINEGAR
Citrus-flavoured vinegars are wonderful for piquant sauces such as hollandaise.

Makes 600ml/1 pint/2½ cups
600ml/1 pint/2½ cups white wine vinegar
rind of 1 lime (preferably unwaxed)
rind of 1 lemon (preferably unwaxed)

Bring the vinegar to the boil in a pan, then pour over the lime and lemon rind in a bowl. Cover and leave to infuse for three days. Strain and pour it into a clean, dry bottle, adding fresh rind for colour.

ROSEMARY VINEGAR
Herb vinegars are excellent for adding flavour to salad dressings and many sauces.

Makes 600ml/1 pint/2½ cups
600ml/1 pint/2½ cups white wine or cider vinegar
90ml/6 tbsp chopped fresh rosemary plus some whole sprigs

Bring the vinegar to the boil in a pan, then pour it over the rosemary in a bowl. Cover and leave to infuse for three days. Strain and pour it into a clean, dry bottle, adding a sprig of rosemary for decoration.

TARRAGON VINEGAR
Make it in exactly the same way as rosemary vinegar, but with tarragon.

Right: *Delicious flavoured vinegars are quick and easy to make.*

Pickles and chutneys

No country store would be complete without a good supply of pickles and chutneys. They are easy to make and the perfect way to deal with a glut of fruit or vegetables. They add a delicious tang to bread and cheese or cold meats, and are always welcome as presents.

KASHMIR CHUTNEY

In the true tradition of the country store, this is a typical family recipe that has been passed down through the generations. It is wonderful with grilled (broiled) sausages.

Makes about 2.75kg/6lb
1kg/2¼lb green apples
15g/½oz garlic cloves
1 litre/1¾ pints/4 cups malt vinegar
450g/1lb/3 cups dates
115g/4oz preserved ginger
450g/1lb/3 cups seeded raisins
450g/1lb/2 cups soft light brown sugar
2.5ml/½ tsp cayenne pepper
25g/1oz salt

Above: *Kashmir chutney.*

1 *Quarter the apples, remove the cores and chop coarsely.*

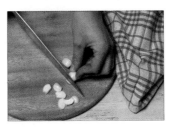

2 *Peel and chop the garlic.*

3 *Place the apple and garlic in a pan with enough vinegar to cover and boil until soft. Chop the dates and ginger and add them to the cooked apple and garlic together with all the other ingredients. Boil gently for 45 minutes. Spoon the mixture into sterilized jars and seal immediately.*

GREEN TOMATO CHUTNEY

Unripened tomatoes are a culinary success rather than a horticultural failure when transformed into a delicious chutney.

Makes about 2.5kg/5¾lb
1kg/2¼lb green tomatoes
450g/1lb apples
2 medium onions
1 litre/1¾ pints/4 cups malt vinegar
450g/1lb/2 cups soft light brown sugar
250g/9oz/1⅔ cups sultanas
  (golden raisins)
7.5ml/1½ tsp mustard powder
5ml/1 tsp ground cinnamon
1.5ml/¼ tsp ground cloves
1.5ml/¼ tsp cayenne pepper

Quarter the tomatoes and place them in a large preserving pan. Quarter, core and chop the unpeeled apples and add them to the tomatoes in the pan. Chop the onions and add them to the tomatoes with all the other ingredients and heat gently, stirring until all the sugar has dissolved. Bring to the boil and simmer uncovered, stirring occasionally, for 1½ hours or until the chutney has thickened. Pour the hot chutney into warm, sterilized jars which should then be sealed immediately.

WINDFALL PEAR CHUTNEY

The seemingly unusable bullet-hard pears that litter the ground beneath old pear trees after high winds respond wonderfully to cooking and can be used to make this easy and tasty chutney.

Makes about 2kg/5lb
*675g/1½lb pears, peeled, chopped
and cored*
225g/8oz onions, chopped
175g/6oz/generous 1 cup raisins
115g/4oz apples, cored and chopped
50g/2oz stem ginger, chopped
115g/4oz/1 cup walnuts, chopped
1 garlic clove, chopped
juice and rind of 1 lemon
600ml/1 pint/2½ cups cider vinegar

*175g/6oz/¾ cup soft light
brown sugar*
2 cloves
5ml/1 tsp salt

Place the prepared pears, onions, raisins, apples, ginger, walnuts, garlic and lemon juice and rind in a large, heatproof mixing bowl. Put the vinegar, sugar, cloves and salt into a large pan. Gently heat, stirring, until

Above: *The merchants who brought spices from India also brought delectable chutney recipes.*

the sugar has dissolved, then bring to the boil briefly and pour over the fruit; cover and leave overnight. In a preserving pan, boil gently for 1½ hours until soft and thickened. Spoon into warmed, sterilized jars and seal.

DILL PICKLES

These piquant pickles are made from prolific outdoor ridge cucumbers.

**Makes three 1 litre/1¾ pint/
   4 cup jars**
675g/1½lb ridge cucumbers
a large bunch fresh dill
5 garlic cloves, peeled and sliced
*900ml/1½ pints/3¾ cups
   white wine vinegar*
45ml/3 tbsp coarse salt
6 black peppercorns
6 white peppercorns
2 bay leaves
1 star anise

Trim the ends off the cucumbers and cut them into 5cm/2in pieces. Place the cucumber in a bowl of cold water, cover and chill for 24 hours.

Above: The full flavour of fruits and vegetables is captured in these colourful and piquant preserves.

Drain the cucumber and, using a wooden cocktail stick (toothpick), pierce each piece in several places. Pack the cucumbers into sterilized jars with the dill and garlic.

Pour the vinegar into a pan with 375ml/13fl oz/1½ cups water, then add the salt, peppercorns, bay leaves and star anise, and bring to the boil for 5 minutes. Remove the pan from the heat, carefully pour the boiling liquid over the cucumbers and seal the jars immediately. If you prefer a sweeter pickle, you can add 45ml/ 3 tbsp sugar to the vinegar mixture in the pan, letting it dissolve before bring the mixture to the boil.

PICKLED PEARS

Pickled pears go especially well with country-cured ham and buttery mashed potatoes.

Makes 1kg/2¼lb
1kg/2¼lb hard pears
juice of 2 lemons
*675g/1½lb/3¼ cups demerara
   (raw) sugar*
1 litre/1¾ pints/4 cups cider vinegar
250ml/8fl oz/1 cup water
3 cinnamon sticks
3 star anise
5ml/1 tsp black peppercorns
5ml/1 tsp whole allspice

Peel the whole pears and immediately toss them in the lemon juice in a bowl to prevent discoloration. Place the pears in a large pan with the remaining ingredients and bring to the boil. Reduce the heat to a simmer and cook until the pears are nearly tender, which should take about 45 minutes.

Spoon the hot pears into sterilized jars and cover with the boiling syrup. Seal immediately.

JACK'S PICKLED SHALLOTS

These shallots have a delicious sweet-sour flavour with none of the harshness that is sometimes associated with pickled onions. If the unpeeled shallots are softened in hot water, they are much easier to peel, and if this is done under water, your eyes will be much less irritated.

Makes about three 500ml/17fl oz/ 2¼ cup jars
675g/1½lb shallots, unpeeled
bay leaves (1 for each jar)
600ml/1 pint/2½ cups malt vinegar
175g/6oz/¾ cup soft light brown sugar
50g/2oz sea salt
10ml/2 tsp pickling spice
7.5ml/½ tbsp balsamic vinegar

Place the shallots in a large bowl and cover with boiling water. Leave for about ten minutes, then remove the shallots from the water and peel them. Pack the shallots into sterilized jars with one bay leaf in each jar.

In a pan, heat the malt vinegar with the sugar, sea salt and pickling spice. Stir until the sugar has completely dissolved, then bring to the boil. Remove from the heat and add the balsamic vinegar.

Pour the vinegar over the shallots and seal the jars immediately. The shallots will be ready in two weeks.

Right: *Preparing shallots becomes less of a chore if they are first blanched in boiling water and then peeled under running water.*

ARTICHOKES IN OLIVE OIL

Artichokes always add a touch of luxury to antipasto and, as one of the few vegetables that are still seasonal, this is a way to enjoy their delicate taste in the winter.

Makes about three 500ml/17fl oz/ 2¼ cup jars
600ml/1 pint/2½ cups white wine vinegar
5ml/1 tsp salt
1kg/2¼lb small artichokes
2 small fresh chillies
5ml/1 tsp black peppercorns
600ml/1 pint/2½ cups virgin olive oil

Put the vinegar, 600ml/1 pint/2½ cups water and salt in a pan. Trim the outer leaves of the artichokes, cut off the tips of the remaining leaves and trim the bases. Place each one in the pan as it is completed or the artichokes will begin to discolour. Boil for about 10 minutes, until tender. Drain, cool and pack them into sterilized jars with the chillies and peppercorns. Cover with the olive oil and seal tightly. Use within six months.

VEGETABLES IN OLIVE OIL

When vegetables are at their luscious best in the garden or at the market, they can be blanched and packed into large jars along with olives and slices of lemon. Covered with good olive oil, they are the next best thing to bottled sunshine.

Quantity depends on amount of vegetables used
selection of vegetables, such as (bell) peppers, aubergines (eggplants), carrots, courgettes (zucchini), mushrooms, broccoli and garlic
green and black olives flavoured with garlic and spices
1 lemon, sliced
bay leaves
virgin olive oil

Cut the vegetables into large, decorative pieces. Blanch each kind separately for 3–4 minutes, then drain well and leave to cool.

Pack the vegetables into a sterilized jar with the olives, lemon and bay leaves, and cover them with olive oil. Seal and use within three months.

Flavoured butters

Butter blended with herbs or other flavourings is delicious spread on fresh bread or as a garnish for grilled (broiled) fish, meat or vegetables.

ROASTED PEPPER BUTTER
Roasting (bell) peppers transforms their flavour; when combined with butter, they make a sweet spread that is ideal for picnics and barbecues.

Makes 115g/4oz/½ cup
1 small red (bell) pepper,
* halved lengthways*
15ml/1 tbsp lemon juice
salt and pepper
115g/4oz/½ cup butter at
* room temperature*
olive oil

Above: *Roasted (bell) pepper butter.*

1 *Grill (broil) the pepper, turning often, until the skin is blackened. Wrap in foil for 10–15 minutes; this helps to loosen its skin.*

2 *Peel the pepper, remove the stalk and pips and slice thinly. Place in the bowl of a food processor or a mortar with the lemon juice and a pinch of salt and pound to a paste.*

3 *Add the butter and seasoning and mix. For a smooth paste, blend in a little olive oil, a teaspoon at a time, until the ingredients hold together.*

HERB BUTTERS
Most herbs can be blended with butter and used to finish cooked dishes. Try mint butter on peas, dill butter on fish, or parsley butter on potatoes. These butters are also delicious when spread on cheese scones, added to stews for a velvety finish, or used as a base for sauces.

Makes 175g/6oz/¾ cup
175g/6oz/¾ cup butter at
* room temperature*
60ml/4 tbsp chopped fresh herbs
salt and pepper

Blend the butter with the herbs and seasoning to taste in a mortar or food processor. Transfer to ramekins and chill for immediate use. Alternatively, spoon the butter on to baking parchment (waxed) paper, roll up into a log and freeze for a couple of hours. Unroll, cut into slices and place in a plastic bag in the freezer ready for use as individual portions. Use within two months for the best flavour.

LIME BUTTER
When topped with lime butter, a dish of simple grilled fish is given a wonderfully exotic flavour.

Makes 115g/4oz/½ cup
finely grated rind of 2 limes
* plus juice of 1 lime*
115g/4oz/½ cup butter at
* room temperature*
salt and pepper

Blend all the ingredients using a food processor or a mortar and pestle and chill for at least 2 hours before using.

GARLIC BUTTER

The most popular of flavoured butters, garlic butter can be used to enliven almost any dish and is the essential ingredient for garlic bread.

Makes 115g/4oz/½ cup

4 garlic cloves
5ml/1 tsp sea salt
15ml/1 tbsp chopped parsley
115g/4oz/½ cup butter at
  room temperature
15ml/1 tbsp lemon juice
salt and pepper

Finely chop the garlic and blend to a paste with the sea salt using a mortar and pestle or the flat of a knife. Blend the garlic paste with the parsley in a bowl, then beat into the butter along with the lemon juice and seasoning to taste. Alternatively, you could mix the ingredients in a food processor. Transfer the garlic butter to ramekins and chill, or freeze in the same way as herb butters (opposite).

ANCHOVY BUTTER

Spread on fingers of wholemeal (whole-wheat) toast, this is a sublime tea-time treat.

Makes 150g/5oz/generous ½ cup

12 anchovy fillets, soaked in milk
  for 1 hour
115g/4oz/½ cup softened butter
juice of 1 lemon
cayenne pepper
black pepper
olive oil

Above: *Crusty French bread and flavoured butters are all the ingredients you need for a delicious and colourful summer lunch, especially when accompanied by richly flavoured olives and a fruity wine.*

Drain the anchovy fillets and, using a mortar and pestle, pound until you have made a paste and then mix with the butter. Season to taste with the lemon juice, cayenne pepper and black pepper and, to give the butter a smooth texture, slowly add a small quantity of olive oil. Finally, pack the butter into a small jar or ramekins if you prefer. Chill in the refrigerator, and be sure to use it within ten days. Alternatively, anchovy butter will freeze very well.

Savoury preserves and sauces

Home-made preserves and sauces are an invaluable and delicious stand-by in the store cupboard (pantry) or larder, and if you have the opportunity to make a few extra pots, they are always very welcome gifts for friends and family.

TRADITIONAL HORSERADISH SAUCE

Everyone who is at all interested in cooking should make horseradish sauce from the fresh root at least once. It is an unforgettable experience, the potent effects of which can be alleviated by keeping the root submerged in water while you scrub and peel it, and by using a food processor to do the fine chopping or grating. However, remember to keep your head averted when you remove the lid of the processor, otherwise the powerful fumes will send you reeling. Do not be put off though: if these simple precautions are observed, the sauce is easy to make and the results are certainly far superior to anything that can be bought in a store. Horseradish sauce is without doubt the essential accompaniment to roast beef and is also delicious with smoked salmon. The thick cream is always added just before serving.

Makes about 200ml/7fl oz/¾ cup
45ml/3 tbsp freshly grated
  horseradish root
15ml/1 tbsp white wine vinegar
5ml/1 tsp caster (superfine) sugar
a pinch of salt
150ml/¼ pint/⅔ cup thick double
  (heavy) cream

Above: *Tomato ketchup and Mint sauce.*

Place the grated horseradish in a bowl, then stir in vinegar, sugar and just a pinch of salt. Pour the sauce into a sterilized jar. It can be kept for up to six months if stored in the refrigerator. A couple of hours before you intend to serve it, stir in the cream and then leave to infuse.

MINT SAUCE

Mint sauce, for many people, is as traditional and inseparable an accompaniment to roast lamb as horseradish sauce is to roast beef, and this simple version keeps very well.

Makes 250ml/8fl oz/1 cup
1 large bunch mint
150ml/¼ pint/⅔ cup wine vinegar
30ml/2 tbsp sugar

Chop the mint finely and place it in a 600ml/1 pint/2½ cup heatproof jug (cup). Pour on 105ml/7 tbsp boiling water and leave to infuse. When the mixture is lukewarm, add the vinegar and sugar. Pour into a bottle and store in the refrigerator. It can be kept for up to six months, but is best within three months.

TOMATO KETCHUP

The real tomato flavour of this home-made version is particularly delicious on hamburgers. An easy method for peeling tomatoes is to open-freeze them (i.e. freeze them on an open rack) overnight, and when they have thawed, the skins should slip off easily.

Makes 2.75kg/6lb
2.25kg/5lb really ripe tomatoes
1 onion
6 cloves
4 allspice berries
6 black peppercorns
1 sprig fresh rosemary
25g/1oz root ginger, sliced
1 celery heart
30ml/2 tbsp soft light brown sugar
65ml/4½ tbsp/⅓ cup raspberry vinegar
  (see page 34)
3 garlic cloves, peeled
15ml/1 tbsp salt

Peel, seed and chop the tomatoes, then place in a large pan. Stud the onion with the cloves, tie it with the allspice, peppercorns, rosemary and ginger into a double layer of muslin (cheesecloth) and add to the pan. Chop the celery, plus the leaves, and add to the pan with the sugar,

raspberry vinegar, garlic and salt. Bring the tomato mixture to the boil over a high heat, stirring occasionally to prevent it sticking. Reduce the heat and simmer for about 1½–2 hours, stirring regularly, until reduced by half. Purée the mixture in a blender or

food mill, then return to the pan and bring to the boil and simmer for about 15 minutes.

Bottle in clean, sterilized jars and store in the refrigerator. Use within two weeks. Alternatively, you can sterilize the ketchup in a water bath

Above: Each of these sauces and preserves is a powerful reduction of the main ingredients.

or oven (see pages 28 and 29) to keep through the winter or for up to 6 months in a cool place.

Flavoured salts and peppers

Flavoured salts and peppers used to be very popular, but they are rarely blended at home these days, as we tend to rely on spice companies to do it for us. This is a pity as they are easy to make, and, when freshly made, have far more flavour than anything that you can buy ready-mixed.

CAYENNE SALT
This adaptation of an old Indian recipe produces flakes of dramatically coloured and wonderfully flavoured salt to use wherever you would normally use cayenne pepper. Remember, however, not to add any additional salt.

Makes 80g/3oz
30ml/2 tbsp sea salt
50g/2oz powdered cayenne pepper
120ml/4fl oz/½ cup white wine

Crush the salt with the cayenne pepper using a mortar and pestle. Add the wine and 250ml/8fl oz/1 cup water to the powdered spices and pour into a bottle. Cork, shake well and stand in a warm place for a week, shaking the mixture from time to

Above: *Sea salt and quails' eggs.*

time. Pour the contents of the bottle into a wide, shallow dish and place in a low oven or a warm place, such as an airing cupboard (linen closet), until all the liquid has evaporated. Scrape the crystals off the base of the dish and leave to stand overnight to allow any residual moisture to evaporate. Store in a sealed glass jar away from light. You could also try making chilli or turmeric salt.

LEMON PEPPER
Dried lemon rind mixed with freshly ground black pepper makes an interesting combination. Try using it on chargrilled fish or in salad dressings.

Makes 125g/4oz
115g/4oz freshly ground coarse
  black pepper
grated rind of two lemons, dried

Mix the two ingredients and store in a sealed glass jar. This is best used within one month, before the flavours begin to fade.

CELERY SALT
This salt is the perfect accompaniment to hard-boiled eggs, especially quails' eggs, which are delicious served as a pre-dinner appetizer with drinks. To make the salt, mix equal amounts of celery seed and sea salt, and leave both whole if you prefer to have a coarser texture, or grind them to a powder using a mortar and pestle if you prefer a finer texture.

MIXED PEPPERCORNS
Black, green, white and pink peppercorns each have their own quite distinctive flavour as well as colour. Mix them together in equal proportions and grind them in the normal way just before use for an exotic flavouring. These will keep for up to one year if left whole.

Right: *A nest of quails' eggs on a leaf plate, surrounded by flavoured salts and peppers.*

Above: *Cayenne salt crystals.*

Herb and spice mixes

Mixed herbs and spices are readily available in the stores, and we tend to accept that these combinations of flavours are the ones to use, but there is no reason why you should not experiment with blending herbs and spices to your own taste. A mortar and pestle are traditionally used to blend the herbs, but using an electric coffee grinder is an easy way to achieve very good results.

LEMON MIX
This combination of lemon flavours makes a wonderful dry marinade for chicken, to be rubbed on to the skin about one hour before roasting or barbecuing.

Makes about 50g/2 oz
2 lemons
30ml/2 tbsp lemon thyme, chopped
15ml/1 tbsp lemon verbena, chopped
15ml/1 tbsp lemon grass, chopped

Above: *Lemon mix.*

1 *Peel the lemons into strips and air dry the rind and herbs on a rack for one to two days.*

2 *When the lemon rind is thoroughly dry, pound it to a powder using a mortar and pestle. Add the other flavourings, then crush and blend them together to the desired texture with the pestle.*

3 *Pack the powdered herbs into attractive fabric bags.*

QUATRE EPICES
This blend of spices is traditionally used in France for flavouring sausages, pâtés and terrines.

7 parts freshly ground black pepper
1 part freshly grated nutmeg
1 part ground cinnamon
1 part ground cloves

Blend the spices together and pack them into a glass jar. Seal tightly and store away from the light. Use within six months.

MIXED SWEET SPICES
The ready-packaged mixed sweet spices that are available are extremely bland compared with a batch that has been freshly ground and blended. Make it in relatively small quantities and, as with the *quatre epices*, store it in sealed containers away from the light and use within six months. It is a good idea to label the spices with the date they were made so that you know when it is time to throw them out and make a fresh batch.

2 parts dried root ginger
1 part white peppercorns or
* allspice berries*
1 part cloves
1 part nutmeg
1 part cinnamon stick

Grind the whole spices and then blend them together.

Right: *Keep your herbs and spices whole and prepare them only when you need them.*

Flavoured mustards

Making your own mustards is surprisingly easy, and just as with other freshly ground spices, the flavour is more intense and aromatic than the ready-made versions.

TARRAGON AND CHAMPAGNE MUSTARD

This delicately flavoured mustard is very good served with cold shellfish or chicken.

Makes about 250g/9oz
30ml/2 tbsp mustard seed
75ml/5 tbsp champagne vinegar
115g/4oz dry mustard powder
115g/4oz/½ cup soft light brown sugar
2.5ml/½ tsp salt
50ml/3½ tbsp virgin olive oil
60ml/4 tbsp chopped fresh tarragon

Soak the mustard seeds overnight in the vinegar. Pour the mixture into the bowl of a blender, add the mustard powder, sugar and salt and blend until smooth. Slowly add the oil while continuing to blend. Stir in the chopped tarragon. Pour the mustard into sterilized jars, seal and store in a cool place.

HONEY MUSTARD

Honey mustard is richly flavoured and is delicious in sauces and salad dressings or drizzled over sausages.

Makes about 500g/1lb 2oz
225g/8oz mustard seeds
15ml/1 tbsp ground cinnamon
2.5ml/½ tsp ground ginger
300ml/½ pint/1¼ cups white wine vinegar
90ml/6 tbsp dark clear honey

Mix the mustard seeds with the spices, pour on the vinegar and then leave to soak overnight. Place the mixture in a mortar and pound until you have made a paste, all the while gradually adding the clear honey. The finished mustard should resemble a stiff paste, so add extra vinegar only if necessary to achieve this. Store the mustard in sterilized jars in the refrigerator. Use within four weeks.

HORSERADISH MUSTARD

Horseradish mustard is a tangy relish that is an excellent accompaniment to cold meats (especially cold beef), smoked fish or strong cheese.

Makes about 400g/14oz
25g/1oz mustard seeds
115g/4oz dry mustard powder
115g/4oz/generous ½ cup sugar
120ml/4fl oz/½ cup white wine or
  cider vinegar
50ml/2fl oz olive oil
5ml/1 tsp lemon juice
30ml/2 tbsp horseradish sauce
  (see page 42)

Place the mustard seeds into a large heatproof bowl and then pour 250ml/8fl oz/1 cup of boiling water over them and leave for 1 hour. Drain the seeds and place in the bowl of a blender with the remaining ingredients. Blend the mixture into a smooth paste and then spoon it into sterilized jars. Store the mustard in the refrigerator and use within three months.

Right: From left: Honey mustard, Horseradish mustard and Tarragon and champagne mustard.

Jams, jellies and honeys

Home-made jams, jellies, curds and flavoured honeys are the perfect way to deal with a glut of fruit and have an intensity of flavour rare in commercial varieties. Some preserving sugars have added pectin, which means that the jellies and jams need to be boiled for only a few minutes to reach setting point. This simplifies the process, gives consistent results and means that it is quite possible to make a pot or two of jam in under half an hour.

An easy way to test for the setting point is to spoon a little of the mixture on to a chilled saucer. If setting point has been reached, a skin will quickly form on the jelly or jam, which will wrinkle when pushed with the finger. Most jams will benefit if left to stand for 15 minutes before being ladled into jars. This ensures that the pieces of fruit are evenly distributed rather than floating on the top. it is best to choose unwaxed fruits for recipes that require the use of lemon rind. Provided jams and jellies are properly sealed, they will keep for a year in the store cupboard or pantry.

CRAB APPLE JELLY

Crab apple trees are so pretty with their abundant flowers and glowing red fruit, and though their role in the garden is mainly decorative, this jelly is a delicious way to make use of the fruit. Serve it with game or use it to glaze an apple tart.

Makes about 1kg/2¼lb from each 600ml/1 pint/2½ cups liquid
1kg/2¼lb crab apples,
3 cloves
preserving sugar

1 Wash the apples and halve them, but do not peel or core.

2 Place the apples and cloves in a pan and cover with water. Bring to the boil, lower the heat and simmer until soft.

3 Strain through muslin (cheesecloth). Warm the sugar in a low oven for 15 minutes. Measure the juice and add 450g/1lb/generous 2 cups of sugar for each 600ml/1 pint/2½ cups of juice. Heat gently, stirring until the sugar dissolves, then boil until setting point is reached. Pour into warmed, sterilized jars; seal.

ROSEHIP AND APPLE JELLY

This recipe uses windfall apples and rosehips gathered from the hedgerows. The resultant jelly is extremely rich in vitamin C as well as full of flavour. It is excellent with scones or crumpets.

Makes about 1kg/2¼lb from each 600ml/1 pint/2½ cups liquid
1kg/2¼lb windfall apples, peeled, trimmed and quartered
450g/1lb firm, ripe rosehips
preserving sugar

Place the apples in a preserving pan with just enough water to cover them, plus 300ml/½ pint/1¼ cups of extra water for the rosehips. Bring to the boil and cook the apples until they are a pulp. Meanwhile, chop the rosehips coarsely in a food processor. Add the rosehips to the cooked apples and leave to simmer for 10 minutes, then remove from the heat and allow to stand for a further ten minutes. Leave the mixture to strain overnight through a thick jelly bag.

Measure the juice and allow 400g/14oz sugar for each 600ml/1 pint/2½ cups of liquid. Warm the sugar in the oven. Bring the juice to the boil and stir in the warmed sugar. Stir the mixture until the sugar has completely dissolved, then leave to boil until the setting point is reached. Finally, pour the jelly into warmed, sterilized jars and seal securely.

Right: *A winter sun illuminates the colours of these appetizing fruit jellies in a glowing richness.*

RHUBARB AND MINT JELLY

This jelly is an unusual alternative to the usual redcurrant or mint jellies that are traditionally served with roast lamb.

Makes about 1kg/2¼lb from each 600ml/1 pint/2½ cups liquid
1kg/2¼lb young rhubarb
preserving sugar
a large bunch fresh mint
30ml/2 tbsp finely chopped fresh mint

Cut the rhubarb into pieces, place in a preserving pan, just cover with water and stew until soft. Strain the fruit through a jelly bag, measure the juice and allow 450g/1lb/generous 2 cups of sugar for each 600ml/1 pint/2½ cups of juice. Warm the sugar in the oven. Pour the juice into a preserving pan, add the bunch of mint and the sugar then bring to the boil, stirring until the sugar has dissolved. Boil to setting point, remove the mint bunch and stir in the chopped mint. Bottle in warm, sterilized jars and seal.

DAMSON JAM

There used to be many damson trees growing wild in the hedgerows. Today they are much scarcer, but if you are fortunate enough to have a supply of damsons, this deeply coloured and richly flavoured jam would grace any tea table.

Makes about 2kg/4¾lb
1kg/2¼lb damsons
1kg/2¼lb/5 cups preserving sugar

Place the damsons in a preserving pan, pour in 1.4 litres/2¼ pints/6 cups water and bring to the boil. Reduce the heat and gently simmer until the damsons are soft.

Meanwhile, warm the sugar in the oven. Stir in the warmed sugar and bring to the boil again, skimming off

Above: *Dried apricot jam.*

the stones (pits) as they rise to the surface (most can be removed this way). Boil to setting point, then leave to stand for 10 minutes. Pour into warm, sterilized jars and seal.

DRIED APRICOT JAM

This is a jam which can be made at any time of year, so when reserves in the store cupboard or pantry start to look low in late winter, make up a batch of apricot jam and dream of summer months to come.

Makes about 2kg/4¾lb
675g/1½lb/3 cups dried apricots
900ml/1½ pints/3¾ cups apple juice made with concentrate
juice and rind of 2 unwaxed lemons
675g/1½lb/3¼ cups preserving sugar
50g/2oz blanched almonds, coarsely chopped

Soak the apricots overnight in the apple juice in a large bowl. Transfer the soaked apricots and juice into a preserving pan and add the lemon juice and rind. Bring the mixture to the boil, lower the heat, then leave to simmer for 15–20 minutes, until the apricots are soft. Meanwhile

warm the sugar in the oven. Add the warmed sugar to the apricots and bring to the boil once more, stirring until the sugar has completely dissolved. Boil until setting point is reached. Stir in the chopped almonds and leave to stand for 15 minutes before bottling in warm, sterilized jars and sealing.

ORANGE MARMALADE

Marmalades have been made since the 15th century, but the early ones were very different to those eaten today. Then they were fruit pastes or 'leathers' while nowadays they are jams made using the peel of citrus fruit. The Seville orange was the only orange available at that time and it was used in all recipes where oranges were required. Today we have a myriad different oranges to use, but the best marmalade is still made with Seville oranges.

Makes about 4kg/9½lb
1kg/2¼lb Seville oranges
1 lemon, unwaxed
1.75kg/4½lb/8¾ cups preserving sugar

Wash and quarter the oranges and the lemon. Remove the flesh, pips and pulp and tie these in a muslin (cheesecloth). Slice the peel, finely or coarsely, whichever is preferred. Place the peel and the muslin bag in a preserving pan and pour on 2.2 litres/4 pints/9 cups water. Bring to the boil, then simmer for 1½–2 hours, until the peel is tender. Meanwhile, warm the sugar in the oven. Stir the sugar into the fruit until it is dissolved, then boil rapidly to setting point. Remove from the heat and leave to stand for 15 minutes. Pour into warm, sterilized jars and seal.

Right: *Clockwise from top left: Orange marmalade, Rhubarb and mint jelly, Damson jam and Dried apricot jam.*

RHUBARB AND GINGER JAM

The best rhubarb for pies and tarts is the young, slender pink spring stems. Later in the summer, when the leaves have reached elephant-ear proportions and the stalks are thick and green, is the time to make this preserve. Use it with cream as a cake filling or stir it into yogurt.

Makes about 2kg/4¾lb

1kg/2¼lb rhubarb
1kg/2¼lb/5 cups preserving sugar
25g/1oz dried root ginger, bruised
115g/4oz crystallized ginger
50g/2oz candied orange peel, chopped

Cut the rhubarb into short pieces and layer with sugar in a glass bowl. Leave overnight. Put the rhubarb and dissolved sugar into a large preserving pan. Tie the bruised ginger root into a piece of muslin (cheesecloth) and add it to the rhubarb. Cook gently for 30 minutes until the rhubarb has softened. Then boil rapidly until the setting point is reached. Remove the muslin. Stir in the crystallized ginger and candied peel, remove from the heat and leave for 15 minutes. Pour the jam into warm, dry, sterilized jars and seal.

LEMON AND LIME CURD

This sumptuously rich fruit curd is definitely not diet food, rather it is a treat to be brought out of the pantry for a special tea time or as a particularly wonderful filling for a roulade.

Makes about 750g/1¾lb

3 large lemons, unwaxed
3 limes, unwaxed
175g/6oz/¾ cup unsalted butter
450g/1lb/2¼ cups granulated (white) sugar
4 large (US extra large) eggs, well beaten

1 Wash the lemons and limes and finely grate the rinds.

2 Squeeze and then strain the juice of the lemons and limes.

3 Melt the butter in a double pan. Add the lemon rind, juice, sugar and well-beaten eggs. Cook the mixture over a gentle heat for about 25 minutes, stirring continuously until it is smooth and thick. Pour the curd into warm, sterilized jars and cover immediately. Use within two months.

Above: *Lemon and lime curd.*

FLAVOURED HONEYS

The finest honeys are those that are made by bees collecting from a single flower source such as clover, lime blossom or wild thyme. These honeys have great character but are also quite expensive. Commercially produced honey can be made a lot more interesting by the simple addition of flavours. The method is extremely easy and the results are truly delicious.

Vanilla Honey

Immerse one split pod of vanilla in a small jar of clear honey. Leave the honey to stand for one week, stirring occasionally, before using.

Ginger Honey

Slice a single piece of preserved stem ginger into a jar of clear honey. Leave for one week, stirring occasionally. It is especially good for a honey-and-lemon drink.

Above: *Curds may be used as a spread on bread but they are also excellent fillings for tarts and roulades, and flavoured honeys make an unusual but delicious preserve.*

Whisky Honey

Gently heat a jar of set honey, stir in 45ml/3 tbsp of whisky and allow the honey to set again. Try it on porridge for a really hearty, celebration breakfast during cold weather.

Candied fruit

Home-made candied fruit bears little or no resemblance in appearance or flavour to the packets of mixed peel available in the supermarket and is so delicious that it can be eaten on its own as a sweetmeat.

CANDIED PEEL RIBBONS

Make this in the latter part of winter when the new season's citrus fruit is available. It will keep all year and can be used in apple pies or baked apples, to enliven a bought mincemeat for mince pies or even added to a beef stew to give a deep, rich flavour. Any syrup that is left over from the candying process can be used in fruit salads or drizzled over a freshly baked vanilla sponge cake. To preserve the individual flavour of each fruit – lemons, limes and oranges – they should all be candied separately. The same process may be used to candy orange slices and larger pieces of citrus peel.

Makes about 675g/1½lb
5 large oranges or 10 lemons or limes, unwaxed
675g/1½lb/3¼ cups granulated (white) sugar, plus extra for sprinkling

Above: *Candied peel ribbons.*

1 *Halve the fruit, squeeze out the juice and discard the flesh, but not the pith.*

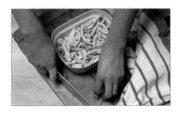

2 *Cut the peel into strips about 1cm/½in wide and place in a pan, cover with boiling water and simmer for 5 minutes. Drain, then repeat this four times, using fresh water each time to remove the peel's bitterness.*

3 *Heat the sugar and 250ml/8fl oz/1 cup water in a heavy pan until the sugar is dissolved. Add the peel and cook, partially covered, until soft (30–40 minutes). Leave to cool then sprinkle with sugar.*

CANDIED GINGER

Now that good-quality fresh root ginger is easily available, it is practical to candy your own. You can use candied ginger in your cakes or desserts, or simply nibble a piece as a treat.

Makes about 675g/1½lb
350g/12oz fresh root ginger
225g/8oz/generous 1 cup granulated (white) sugar
caster (superfine) sugar, for coating

Place the ginger in a pan and then cover with water and boil gently for about 15 minutes until tender. Drain the ginger thoroughly and peel when cool. Cut into 5mm/¼in slices.

In a heavy pan, dissolve the sugar in 120ml/4fl oz/½ cup of water and cook, without stirring, over a low heat until the mixture becomes syrupy, which should take about 15 minutes. Add the ginger slices and continue to cook over a low heat, occasionally shaking the pan to prevent the ginger sticking, until the ginger has absorbed the syrup. Remove the ginger slices, place them on a wire rack and leave them to cool.

When they are cool enough, coat the ginger slices with the sugar and spread them out on baking parchment (waxed) paper for two to three days, until the sugar has crystallized. Store them in an airtight glass jar, where they will keep for 2–3 months.

Right: *Citrus fruit can be candied whole or in ribbons or slices, but however it is done, it is twice as good when home-made.*

Preserved fruit

There is great pleasure to be gained from admiring well-stocked store cupboard or pantry shelves, laden with bottled fruit and vegetables. They are beautiful to look at and each holds the promise of pleasure to come.

BOTTLED FRUIT IN SYRUP

Always choose good-quality, unbruised fruit for bottling. The quantity of syrup required depends on the type of fruit and whether it is whole or sliced. Soft fruit needs less syrup than hard fruit, but as a general guide, the syrup should just cover the fruit. Unused syrup can be stored in the refrigerator until needed. The washed fruit is first poached in a syrup made from 225g/8oz/generous 1 cup sugar to every 600ml/1 pint/2½ cups water. If a heavier syrup is required, the proportion of sugar can be increased to up to 450g/1lb/2¼ cups to each 600ml/1 pint/2½ cups. The fruit is then packed into hot, sterilized bottles,

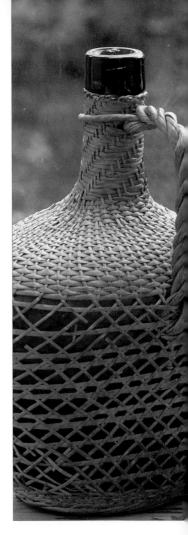

Above: *Ripe peaches and apricots.*

covered with syrup just off the boil and sealed immediately. Bottled fruit is best stored in a dark, or at least dim, cool place.

BRANDIED PEACHES

The time to make this luxurious preserve is in high summer when the fruit is at its cheapest and most flavoursome. There is no need to use your finest brandy either; something quite rough and ready will become ambrosial when mixed with the peaches and their syrup.

Makes 1.75kg/4½lb peaches, plus syrup

1.75kg/4½lb/8¾ cups sugar
2 cinnamon sticks
15ml/1 tbsp cloves
1.75kg/4½lb ripe but firm peaches, scalded and peeled
400ml/14 fl oz/1⅔ cups brandy

In a large pan, dissolve the sugar in 600ml/1 pint/2½ cups water over a gentle heat. Break up the cinnamon sticks, tie them in a piece of muslin (cheesecloth) with the cloves and add them to the sugar water. Bring to the boil, add the peaches a few at a time and simmer each batch for 5 minutes until the peaches are just tender. Drain the cooked peaches, pouring the syrup back into the pan.

When all the peaches are cooked, boil the syrup until it has thickened slightly. Allow it to cool for 10 minutes. Stir the brandy into the syrup. Pack the peaches into hot, sterilized bottles and cover with the brandy syrup. Seal the bottles immediately and leave for 2 weeks before using.

CHERRIES IN EAU DE VIE

These cherries should be consumed with caution as they pack quite a punch. Serve them with chocolate torte or as a wicked garnish to a rice pudding.

Makes 450g/1lb cherries, plus syrup

450g/1lb ripe cherries
8 blanched almonds
90ml/6 tbsp sugar
500ml/17fl oz/2¼ cups eau de vie

Wash and pit the cherries and then pack them with the almonds into a sterilized, wide-necked bottle. Spoon the sugar over the fruit, then cover with the eau de vie and seal securely. Store for a month before using them, and shake the bottle every now and then to help dissolve the sugar.

SPICED PEARS

Similar to pickled pears, this conserve is for eating with cold meats. It is especially good with ham, pork or gammon (smoked or cured ham).

Makes 1kg/2¼lb
600ml/1 pint/2½ cups red
  wine vinegar
rind of 1 lemon
4cm/1½in piece fresh root ginger
1 cinnamon stick
10ml/2 tsp whole allspice berries
1 bay leaf
450g/1lb/2¼ cups sugar
1kg/2¼lb hard pears
cloves

Pour the vinegar into a large preserving pan, add the lemon rind, all the spices,

Above: *Spiced pears.*

except the cloves, and the bay leaf. Dissolve the sugar in the vinegar over a low heat.

Peel the pears, leaving them whole, stick a clove into each one and add them to the vinegar in the pan. Simmer gently until the pears are tender and transparent. Lift them out with a slotted spoon and pack them into hot, sterilized jars. Boil the syrup until thickened and pour it over the pears, sealing immediately.

Bottled vegetables

With fresh vegetables available all year, we no longer need to rely on bottled vegetables as previous generations did, but they are still a good store-cupboard standby, and with the addition of herbs and spices, are turned from a staple to a luxury item.

BOTTLED CHERRY TOMATOES

Cherry tomatoes bottled in their own juices with garlic and basil are sweetly delicious and a perfect accompaniment to thick slices of country ham.

Makes 1kg/2¼lb
1kg/2¼lb cherry tomatoes
5ml/1 tsp salt per 1 litre/1¾ pint/
4 cup jar
5ml/1 tsp sugar per 1 litre/1¾ pint/
4 cup jar
fresh basil
5 garlic cloves per jar

Above: *Bottled cherry tomatoes.*

1 *Prick each tomato with a cocktail stick (toothpick).*

2 *Pack the tomatoes into clean dry jars, adding the salt and sugar as you go.*

3 *Fill the jars to within 2cm/¾in of the top. Tuck in the basil and garlic. Rest the lids on the jars and stand on a baking tray lined with newspaper in a 120°C/ 250°F/Gas ½ oven. After 45 minutes, when the juice is simmering, remove from the oven and seal. Use within six months.*

PICKLED BEETROOT

Next time you decide to bake some potatoes, add a pan of beetroots (beets) to the oven and use them to make a pickle, which will make a welcome change to the usual boiled variety – the flavour will be richer and earthier. If you are boiling the beetroots, cook them in their skins and leave them to cool in the cooking liquid and then gently rub off their skins. If you prefer, you can also use pre-cooked beetroot bought from the supermarket for this pickle.

Makes 450g/1lb
450g/1lb beetroot (beet), cooked
1 large onion, sliced
300ml/½ pint/1¼ cups cider vinegar
50g/2oz/¼ cup sugar
a few strips fresh
  horseradish (optional)

Slice the beetroot and pack it into a jar, layering it with the sliced onion. Pour the vinegar and 150ml/¼ pint/ ⅔ cup water into a pan. Add the sugar and horseradish (if using) and bring to the boil. Pour the liquid over the beetroot and seal the jar. Store in a cool place and use within one month, or longer if kept in the refrigerator.

PICKLED RED CABBAGE

This pickle is especially good served with bread and cheese or slices of cold duck or goose, as the acidity cuts the richness.

Makes 1–1.5kg/2¼–3½lb
675g/1½lb shredded red cabbage
1 large Spanish (Bermuda)
  onion, sliced

25g/1oz/2 tbsp sea salt
600ml/1 pint/2½ cups red
  wine vinegar
75g/3oz/6 tbsp soft light brown sugar
15ml/1 tbsp coriander seeds
3 cloves
2.5cm/1in piece fresh root ginger
1 star anise
2 bay leaves
4 eating apples

Mix the sliced cabbage and onion thoroughly with the salt, place in a colander and allow to drain overnight.

Rinse and take the excess water off the vegetables using a clean cloth. Pour the vinegar into a pan, add the sugar, spices and bay leaves. Bring to the boil then allow to cool.

Core and coarsely chop the apples and then layer them with the cabbage

Above: *Bottled young, succulent vegetables can be as delicious as freshly picked ones.*

and onions in clean, dry preserving jars. Pour on the cooled spiced vinegar (strain out the spices if you prefer a milder pickle), seal and store for a week before eating. Best eaten within two months.

Syrups, cordials and liqueurs

There is a freshness and intensity of flavour in home-made syrups, cordials and liqueurs that is very rarely present in their commercial counterparts. They will keep wonderfully from year to year in your store cupboard or pantry and may be used as flavourings for home-made ice creams and sorbets as well as for making delicious drinks.

ROSEHIP SYRUP
Rosehips are a rich source of vitamin C, so this is an ideal winter drink to ward off coughs and colds.

**Makes about 750ml/1¼ pints/
3 cups per 600ml/1 pint/
2½ cups syrup**
ripe but firm rosehips
granulated (white) sugar

Wash the rosehips thoroughly, then top and tail them. Place them in a food processor and chop coarsely. Tip them into a pan, barely cover with water and bring to the boil. Turn down the heat and leave to simmer gently for about 10 minutes, until tender. Remove from the heat and then allow to stand for a further 10 minutes. Leave to strain overnight through a thick jelly bag. The juice should be clear. However, if it is not, strain it through several thicknesses of muslin (cheesecloth) to remove any remaining particles. Measure the juice. For each 600ml/1 pint/2½ cups, add 350g/12oz/1¾ cups sugar. Boil until the syrup thickens and then pour into warm, dry, sterilized bottles and seal securely with a cork. To drink, dilute the syrup to taste with water.

ELDERFLOWER CORDIAL
The rank scent of the elderflower bush gives no clue to the delicate flavour of this cordial made from its flowers. It makes a wonderfully refreshing summer drink and a delicious sorbet. A spoonful of the cordial added to cooked gooseberries gives them a subtle muscatel flavour.

Makes 2.5 litres/4¼ pints/10¼ cups
*1.5kg/3½lb/7½ cups granulated
(white) sugar*
50g/2oz citric acid
*25 elderflower heads, washed and
gently shaken dry*
2 lemons, unwaxed, sliced

Dissolve the sugar in 1.5 litres/2½ pints/6¼ cups hot water and leave to cool. When cool, stir in the citric acid and

Above: *Rosehip syrup and Elderflower cordial.*

Right: *Syrups and cordials are a delicious alternative to commercial squashes.*

add the elderflowers and lemons. Cover and leave to infuse for two days, stirring occasionally. Strain and pour into clean, dry, sterilized bottles and seal. Store in a cool place to avoid the possibility of slight fermentation taking place. To serve, dilute to taste with still or sparkling mineral water. Will keep indefinitely in a cool place.

ELDERBERRY SYRUP
The elder bush is very generous with its bounty. Not only is it laden with foaming white flowers in the early summer, but it also hangs heavy with purple berries in the autumn. The berries are ripe when the heads hang down. Elderberry syrup is a traditional country treatment for coughs and colds.

**Makes about 750ml/1¼ pints/
3 cups per 600ml/1 pint/
2½ cups syrup**
ripe elderberries
granulated (white) sugar
cinnamon sticks

Wash the heads of the elderberries thoroughly, remove the stalks and then place the berries in a large earthenware pot. Cover and bake in a moderately hot oven at 190°C/375°F/Gas 5 until the juice runs. Strain off the juice into a pan. For each 600ml/1 pint/2½ cups, add 225g/8oz/generous 1 cup sugar and a broken up stick of cinnamon.

Cover the pan and boil the mixture gently until the syrup thickens. Pour the syrup into warm, dry, sterilized bottles and seal securely. To serve, just dilute to taste with hot water.

PEACH WINE

This is not really a proper wine at all, but instead a delicious and refreshing amalgam of peaches, wine and eau de vie. Although you could drink it at any time of the year, it is really intended to be made and drunk during the summer, either on its own or diluted with soda water.

Makes about 1.2 litres/2 pints/ 5 cups

6 ripe peaches
1 litre/1¾ pints/4 cups dry white wine
200g/7oz/1 cup caster (superfine) sugar
175ml/6fl oz/¾ cup eau de vie

1 *Peel and halve the peaches, then poach them in the white wine for about 15 minutes, until tender. Cover and allow to stand overnight.*

2 *Remove the peaches, then strain the liquid through a coffee filter. Add the sugar and eau de vie and stir to dissolve the sugar.*

3 *Pour the wine into clean, dry, sterilized bottles and cork. Store in the refrigerator. Drink within two weeks. Serve chilled.*

Above: *Peach wine.*

MULBERRY RATAFIA

Several years ago, I was lucky enough to have a glut of mulberries and I transformed some of the fruit into this delicious drink. There are still a couple of bottles left and the fresh mulberry taste has not diminished at all over the years.

Quantity depends on the amount of fruit picked

mulberries
caster (superfine) sugar
vodka, brandy or gin

Fill clean, dry sterilized jars with clean fruit. Pour in caster sugar so that it comes a third of the way up the jar, then fill to the top with the spirit of your choice. Seal the jars and shake them to help the sugar dissolve. Store for at least a couple of months, occasionally shaking the jars.

Strain off the fruit (which you can use to make a delicious apple pie) and bottle the ratafia in clean, dry, sterilized bottles and seal securely. It should keep indefinitely if stored in airtight bottles.

SLOE GIN

This is a real country drink, which was traditionally used to celebrate high days and holidays. Sloes are gathered from the hedgerows after the first frosts and the first bottle is ready in time for Christmas.

Quantity depends on the amount of fruit picked

sloes
caster (superfine) sugar
gin

Wash the sloes, removing any stalks, bits of twig or leaves. Prick each sloe with a cocktail stick (toothpick) or needle, then pack the fruit into a wide-necked jar or bottle. Pour in caster sugar so that it comes halfway up the jar, then fill to the top with gin and seal. Shake the jar from time to time to help the sugar dissolve. Before drinking, strain off the sloes and decant the sloe gin into a pretty bottle that is clean and dry.

Right: *Delicious and colourful liqueurs made from fruit.*

Teas and tisanes

Before tea was widely available, country people made hot drinks from the herbs growing wild and in their gardens, and found them to be good for their health as well as pleasant tasting. With the arrival of teas from China, they followed the example of the Chinese and added flowers and other flavourings to enhance the taste and appearance of the teas.

ROSE PETAL TEA

Another delicious drink for summer, this one is very pretty when poured unstrained into tea glasses so that the petals and tea leaves are visible at the bottom of the glass.

Makes 130g/4½oz
15g/½oz scented red rose petals
115g/4oz Oolong tea

Mix the rose petals with the tea and store in an airtight container.

Above: *Marigold and verbena tisane.*

MARIGOLD AND VERBENA TISANE

This attractive and distinctive gold and green tisane is reputed to be excellent for purifying the blood and aiding digestion. Why not try drinking some after a heavy meal? The verbena gives the tea an intensely lemony flavour and the marigold adds a peppery note.

Makes 75g/3oz
50g/2oz dried marigold petals
25g/1oz dried lemon
*   verbena leaves*

Mix the petals and leaves together and then store in an airtight container. To serve, all you have to do is infuse one tablespoon of the tea in a mug of hot water, then leave it to stand, covered, for about 5 minutes before drinking.

ORANGE AND LEMON TEA

Citrus fruit adds a fresh zestiness to tea and this blend, with its addition of dried orange and lemon rind, is ideal for drinking without milk on a summer's afternoon. For an even more pronounced flavour, a few drops of orange and lemon essential oils can be mixed into the tea.

Above: *Rose petal tea.*

Makes 130g/4½oz
1 lemon, unwaxed
1 orange
115g/4oz Ceylon tea

Peel the orange and the lemon, cut the rind into fine ribbons then allow it to dry slowly in a warm place. Mix the dried rind with the tea and store in an airtight container.

CHAMOMILE AND PEPPERMINT TISANE

This is perfect as a bedtime drink, as chamomile is a gentle sedative and peppermint is an excellent aid to digestion.

Makes 100g/3½oz
75g/3oz chamomile flowers
25g/1oz dried peppermint leaves

Above: *These teas and tisanes can be easily blended from home-grown herbs and flowers.*

Mix, store and prepare this tisane in the same way as the marigold and verbena tisane above. For the best results, always prepare your tisanes with hot, not boiling water and cover them while they steep.

Baked goods and breads

Tea time is often more than a just a quick cup of tea and a chat for most country people; it is a real feast with platefuls of teabreads and delicious cakes to stave off the hunger brought on by lots of fresh air and exercise.

APPLE CAKE

This wholesome and delicious cake is ideal for ravenously hungry children who have just come home from school.

Makes 12 generous slices
115g/4oz/½ cup butter
115g/4oz/½ cup soft light
* brown sugar*
2 eggs, beaten
150g/5oz/1¼ cups wholemeal
* (whole-wheat) flour*
5ml/1 tsp baking powder
apple juice, for mixing
2 large eating apples, cored
15ml/1 tbsp demerara
* (raw) sugar*
5ml/1 tsp ground cinnamon

Preheat the oven to 190°C/375°F/ Gas 5. Cream the butter and sugar until they are soft and fluffy. Then gradually beat in the eggs. Mix the flour and baking powder and add them alternately with the apple juice until you have a batter of dropping consistency. Spread the batter in a greased Swiss roll tin (jelly roll pan). Slice the apples into crescents and arrange them in rows on the batter. Sprinkle with the sugar and cinnamon. Put in the oven and bake for 30 minutes. Allow to cool, then cut into wedges.

COURGETTE TEABREAD

The advantage, and disadvantage, of having your own courgette (zucchini) plants is the way they seem to be able to grow a new crop overnight. Eventually, even the most enthusiastic of courgette eaters will begin to groan every time another dish featuring the courgettes appears. However, this teabread is a cunning and delicious way to disguise the courgettes and will win the approval of even the most vegetable-phobic child. It also keeps well.

Makes two 450g/1lb cakes
2 eggs
225g/8oz/generous 1 cup sugar
250ml/8fl oz/1 cup peanut or corn oil
450g/1lb courgettes (zucchini), grated
350g/12oz/3 cups plain
* (all-purpose) flour*
5ml/1 tsp salt
1.5ml/¼ tsp baking powder
5ml/1 tsp bicarbonate of soda
* (baking soda)*
5ml/1 tsp ground cinnamon
chopped walnuts, for sprinkling

Preheat the oven to 180°C/350°F/ Gas 4. Beat the eggs until light and fluffy. Add the sugar, oil and grated courgettes and mix well to make a batter. Sift the dry ingredients and mix them thoroughly into the batter. Add the chopped walnuts. Pour the mixture into two greased and floured 450g/1lb loaf tins (pans) and bake for 1 hour until the bread is well risen and brown. Serve sliced and buttered.

BOILED FRUIT CAKE

The name refers to the fact that the mixed dried fruit is cooked with the butter, sugar and tea before the cake is baked. This is an extremely easy cake to make and keeps extremely well.

Makes a 450g/1lb cake
350g/12oz/2 cups mixed dried fruit
115g/4oz ½ cup butter
115g/4oz/½ cup soft light brown sugar
150ml/¼ pint/⅔ cup strong black tea
1 egg, beaten
225g/8oz/2 cups self-raising
* (self-rising) flour*

Preheat the oven to 180°C/350°F/ Gas 4. Place the dried fruit, butter, sugar and tea in a pan, bring to the boil and then simmer for 20 minutes. Remove from the heat and allow to cool. Stir in the beaten egg and flour. Pour the mixture into a greased 450g/1lb loaf tin (pan) and bake for 1½ hours.

Right: *Clockwise from top left: Courgette (zucchini) teabread, Boiled fruit cake, Apple cake, Yorkshire parkin and Bread pudding.*

Above: *Courgette (zucchini) teabread.*

BREAD PUDDING

This is a traditional recipe for using up stale bread to make a tasty, sustaining snack or dessert.

Serves 6–8

225g/8oz stale bread
300ml/½ pint/1¼ cups milk
115g/4oz/⅔ cup mixed dried fruit
50g/2oz/¼ cup butter, melted
90g/3½oz/½ cup sugar
15ml/1 tbsp mixed (apple pie) spice
1 egg, beaten with 60ml/4 tbsp milk
a pinch of grated nutmeg

Preheat the oven to 180°C/350°F/Gas 4. Break up the bread and place it in a mixing bowl. Pour on the milk and leave to soak. When the bread is soft, add the dried fruit, melted butter, sugar and spice and beat well. Stir in the egg and milk mixture. Pour into a greased ovenproof dish and sprinkle with the nutmeg. Bake for about 45 minutes, until set.

MALT BREAD

Another favourite tea-time treat with children, this deliciously gooey malt bread is perfect when friends come home from school for tea.

Makes two 450g/1lb loaves

450g/1lb/4 cups whole-wheat flour
2.5ml/½ tsp salt
25g/1oz good-quality mixed spices
  (see page 46)
50g/2oz/4 tbsp muscovado
  (molasses) sugar
25g/1oz fresh yeast
15ml/1 tbsp malt extract
25g/1oz/¼ cup soya flour
15ml/1 tbsp sunflower oil
115g/4oz/⅔ cup raisins
1 egg, lightly beaten with a little salt
For the glaze
15ml/1 tbsp malt extract
15ml/1 tbsp concentrated apple juice

Mix together the flour, salt, spices and sugar in a large bowl. In another bowl, mix the yeast with the malt extract, soya flour and 300ml/½ pint/1¼ cups warm water, and leave to ferment in a warm place for 5 minutes or until the surface is quite frothy. Add the ferment with the oil to the dry ingredients. Mix well with a wooden spoon and then knead for 5–7 minutes. Lightly knead in the raisins and transfer to a clean bowl. Leave to rise for 30 minutes, covered with a damp dish cloth. Knock back

(punch down) the dough, knead lightly and divide between two greased 450g/1lb loaf tins (pans). Leave to rise for 30 minutes. Preheat the oven to 200°C/400°F/Gas 6. Brush the top of the loaves with the beaten egg and bake for 30–35 minutes. While still hot, brush the loaves with a mixture of malt extract and apple juice.

WHOLEMEAL LOAF

Breadmaking is wonderfully therapeutic: the kneading and the delicious aroma of baking bread are very calming.

Makes two 450g/1lb loaves

7.5ml/1½ tsp dried yeast
2.5ml/½ tsp sugar
450g/1lb/4 cups wholemeal
  (whole-wheat) bread flour
5ml/1 tsp malt extract or molasses
5ml/1 tsp salt
15ml/1 tbsp oil
sunflower seeds or rolled oats,
  for sprinkling

Activate the yeast by adding the sugar and 150ml/¼ pint/⅔ cup warm water. This will take about 10 minutes. Place the flour in a warmed bowl and make a well in the centre. Mix the malt or molasses and the salt with 150ml/¼ pint/⅔ cup warm water and pour into the well. Add the activated yeast mixture and mix well by hand. Turn on to a floured surface and knead for about 3 minutes, until the dough becomes elastic. Divide into two pieces, fold each piece in three and place in two greased 450g/1lb loaf tins (pans). Cover with a clean dish towel and leave in a warm place until the dough is well risen.
   Preheat the oven to 200°C/400°F/Gas 6. Sprinkle the loaves with sunflower seeds or rolled oats and place in the top of the oven. Bake for

Left: *Wholemeal (whole-wheat) loaf.*

10 minutes, then reduce the heat to 180°C/350°F/Gas 4 and bake for a further 30–40 minutes. Take the loaves out of the oven, remove one from the tin and tap the base: if the bread is cooked it should sound hollow.

PLAITED HERB LOAF

Flavoured breads are wonderful served with soups and salads. They taste best of all when made with fresh herbs and eaten in the garden in the summer sunshine.

Makes a 450g/1lb plait (braid)
5ml/1 tsp dried yeast
450g/1lb/4 cups strong white bread flour
5ml/1 tsp salt
150ml/¼ pint/⅔ cup warm milk
30ml/2 tbsp olive oil or garlic-
 flavoured oil
15ml/1 tbsp finely chopped fresh herbs
 of your choice
beaten egg, for brushing

Sprinkle the yeast on 150ml/¼ pint/⅔ cup warm water and leave to activate for about 10 minutes. Then mix the flour and salt in a warmed mixing bowl. Make a well in the centre and add the yeast mixture with the milk, oil and herbs. Mix by hand to a soft dough. Turn the dough on to a well-floured surface and knead for about 10 minutes, until the dough becomes elastic. Return the dough to the bowl, cover and leave it to rise for about 1 hour, until it has doubled in size.

   Knock back (punch down) the dough and knead lightly. Divide into three pieces, roll them into ropes and plait (braid) together. Carefully lift the plait on to a greased baking sheet, brush with the beaten egg and sprinkle with some extra herbs. Cover and leave to rise for 30 minutes. Preheat the oven to 220°C/425°F/Gas 7. Bake the loaf for 35–40 minutes.

Right: A herb loaf, Wholemeal (whole-wheat) loaves and Malt bread.

71

Sweetmeats and candies

Most modern children have no idea that sweets and candies can actually be made at home. You will be viewed as something akin to a magician, and become just as popular, if you produce some of these delicious confections from your pantry.

COCONUT ICE
A coconut used to be a rare and precious treat in the country. Often the only way to get hold of one was to win it at the travelling fair. The trophy was borne home by the victor to be transformed into delectable coconut ice, which would be parcelled up into little squares and taken to school to share with friends. The squares can be wrapped in individual cellophane parcels.

Makes 16 x 5cm/2in squares
1 coconut
450g/1lb/2¼ cups sugar
coconut milk, from the coconut,
   about 120ml/4fl oz/½ cup
25g/1oz/2 tbsp butter
red food colouring

Above: *Coconut ice.*

1 *Break open the coconut, reserving the milk, and grate the coconut flesh. Place the sugar, coconut milk and butter in a pan and gently bring to the boil.*

2 *Slowly stir in the grated coconut and continue boiling for 10 minutes. It is important to keep stirring all the time.*

3 *Divide the mixture between two bowls and colour one portion pink. Then press the uncoloured coconut mixture into a layer in a greased 20cm/8in square tin (pan), and cover it with a layer of pink coconut. Leave to set and then cut into squares.*

CHOCOLATE AND WALNUT FUDGE
Children love to get involved in fudge making, and with any luck, by the time they have licked the bowl and the spoon, they will have the patience to wait for it to be properly cool before devouring it all.

Makes 16 x 5cm/2in squares
450g/1lb/2¼ cups granulated
   (white) sugar
90ml/6 tbsp single (light) cream
25g/1oz/2 tbsp unsalted butter, softened
175g/6oz plain (semisweet)
   chocolate, grated
walnut halves

Butter a 20cm/8in square tin (pan). In a large, heavy pan, mix the sugar and cream together until you have made a thick paste, then add the butter and chocolate and stir well. Place the mixture over a gentle heat and stir it until all the ingredients have completely melted and thoroughly blended.

Then raise the heat and boil for 5 minutes while stirring constantly. Finally, remove from the heat, beat the mixture hard until it thickens, then pour it into the prepared tin. Before the fudge has completely cooled, cut it into squares and place a half walnut on each square.

HOME-MADE TRUFFLES

Making truffles at home is easier than you think and can be great fun for all the family. However, they are fairly rich and are definitely something of a treat to be brought out on special occasions. They freeze very successfully if you want to keep some back for another occasion.

Makes 20 truffles

225g/8oz plain (semisweet) chocolate,
  preferably 70% cocoa solids
75g/3oz/6 tbsp unsalted butter
1 egg yolk
unsweetened cocoa powder,
  for dusting

Above: *Home-made sweets and candies may be a wicked indulgence in these health-conscious days, but everyone deserves a treat now and then.*

Break the chocolate up into squares and melt it with the butter in a double boiler, stirring at the end to make sure that they are thoroughly blended. Remove from the heat, cool slightly, and beat in the egg yolk. Chill the mixture until it is firm enough to shape, then roll the mixture into balls and roll these in the cocoa powder. Place each truffle in a paper case. Keep them in the refrigerator and use within one week.

The Bathroom

A selection of traditional creams, lotions and other natural beauty products to pamper your skin.

Making cosmetics

osmetics is another area of our modern life that we have handed over to the 'experts'. While it is true that many of today's products are more pleasing in texture and smell than earlier creams and lotions, it is also true that they are nearly all made from the same, easily obtainable basic ingredients and that we are paying more for the packaging than for the contents. It can also be rewarding using home-made creams and lotions. The simplest of the techniques in this section involves the mixing of like with like, for example diluting a herbal infusion with rosewater, or blending a carrier oil with essential oils.

CHOOSING AND USING SAFE INGREDIENTS
I have tried to ensure that all the ingredients in this section are readily available. Inevitably, some are harder to find than others, but your local pharmacist may be prepared to order these for you. Dried herbs can be bought by mail order (see list of suppliers, pages 156 and 157). When buying essential oils, it is very important that you purchase from companies with established reputations, as oils can vary enormously in quality. Although the ingredients in this section have been chosen with safety in mind, it is advisable to do a patch test with the cream or lotion before using it.

Left: *To test that your home-made cosmetics do not cause an allergic reaction, spread a small amount on your inner arm and leave for 24 hours to see whether there is an adverse reaction, such as a rash.*

WARNING: Certain essential oils should not be handled by pregnant women or anyone who may be pregnant or where there is an existing medical condition. If in any doubt, seek advice from your medical practitioner. Wear rubber gloves when handling the concentrated oil and spice blends to avoid any irritation.

TO MAKE A HERBAL INFUSION
Herbal infusions are very easy to make and are delicious to drink – either hot or cold. Always store them in a cool place or refrigerator. You can also make infusions from flowers. Mix these with rosewater or witch hazel to make soothing or refreshing skin tonics (see page 92).

Makes 1 cup
25g/1oz dried herbs or flowers or 50g/2oz fresh herbs or flowers

1 *Place the herbs or flowers in a heatproof jug (pitcher). If you prefer, you can mix herbs or flowers together, but ensure the total quantity is the same.*

2 *Pour 475ml/16fl oz/2 cups boiling water over the herbs or flowers. Cover the jug with a lid or sterilized gauze and allow to cool at room temperature.*

3 *Strain the liquid into a sterilized bottle and seal. A jug with a tight-fitting lid would do. Store in the refrigerator and consume or use within two to three days.*

MAKING CREAMS AND LOTIONS

Creams and lotions are slightly more complicated than a herbal infusion as they involve making an emulsion, which is basically a mixture of oil and water made with a whisk.

You will find it easier to make your own creams and lotions if you have scales, a measuring jug (cup) and spoons that can accurately measure small amounts. It is advisable to keep the equipment used for cosmetics separate from cooking utensils as the residues of oils and waxes may taint your cooking. A double boiler is essential for melting waxes because direct heat will burn them.

Once you have blended your oils and made your creams and lotions, store them in glass or china containers, rather than plastic ones, as the essential oils

Above: *Waxes such as white and yellow beeswax and carnauba are essential ingredients in many cosmetics.*

Left: *Keep your home-made cosmetics in coloured glass bottles to prevent light from affecting them.*

can migrate into plastic. Ideally the containers should be made of coloured glass and always stored away from sunlight to preserve the oils in good condition.

Herbs and flowers for health and beauty

It is advisable to use organically grown herbs and flowers whenever possible. Many herbs and flowers are safe to use and it is unusual to have an allergic reaction, but if you are in doubt, carry out a patch test (see page 76). Anyone who is taking homeopathic remedies should not use any of the mint family during treatment as they interfere with the action of the remedies.

When selecting your own herbs for use, fresh or dried, pick them in the morning on a dry day before they reach the flowering stage. If you are drying the herbs for later use, they should be hung upside down, covered by brown paper bags or cones of newspaper. Once fully dry, they must be stripped from their stems and stored in dark glass jars away from any source of heat.

ORANGE FLOWER WATER
AND ROSEWATER

Orange flower water and rosewater are used in many lotions and creams. In the Middle East they are considered to enhance health and beauty, and are drunk extremely diluted. They are a by-product of the perfume industry, obtained by distillation. The quality can vary enormously, but price is a general guide and the best rosewater is 'triple distilled'. Be cautious about very fancy bottles, which are sometimes used to disguise an inferior product.

Above: *To ensure that you gather lavender in its very best condition, you should pick it before noon on a dry and sunny day. In this way the herb will retain the full intensity of its aromatic qualities (this applies to all herbs). It can then be tied into bundles and hung up to dry somewhere cool and airy.*

Left: *All fresh herbs, but especially those that have been grown organically, are wonderful, fragrant ingredients to use in all kinds of natural beauty products. They are also extremely rewarding when used to scent the bath. Simply add a few fresh leaves to hot water, leave for 5 minutes, then enjoy.*

Right: *A very useful tip is to tie paper cones around your bundles of herbs, such as thyme, marjoram and oregano, in order to keep them free of dust and also to make sure that the plants retain their colour while they are drying.*

Essential oils

The fruits, herbs and flowers described here have been used in the bathroom projects in this book. It is important to double the dilution of any oil for use on children and babies.

HERB OILS

Lavender: Wonderfully therapeutic, this oil can be used undiluted on the skin to treat cuts and burns. Used in oils and lotions, it relieves headaches and aids rest and relaxation.

Tea tree: Derived from an Australian shrub called the ti-tree, which has long been used by the Aborigine people as a valuable healing herb, tea tree oil (as it is more commonly known) is an antiseptic oil that is good for skin complaints.

Peppermint: This powerfully aromatic oil should be used sparingly or it may overwhelm. Peppermint tea is the best herbal treatment for digestive problems.

Patchouli: The oil of this plant has an uplifting effect and is excellent for use on more mature and problem skins.

Rosemary: Stimulating and invigorating, rosemary oil is one of the best treatments for any scalp problems. However, do not use during pregnancy.

Chamomile: A gentle healing oil, which also soothes and relaxes, chamomile is a good treatment for most skin conditions and is used to promote hair and scalp health.

FRUIT OILS

Lemon: Lemon oil has both valuable antibacterial and astringent qualities, and may be incorporated into remedies in the treatment of oily skin. It can irritate, however, and so should be used only in 1% dilution. Nor should it be applied to the skin before going out into direct sunlight, because it can cause skin discoloration.

Orange: Like the fruit itself, this warm golden oil imparts a wonderful sense of well-being and relaxation. Incorporated into skin-care preparations, it refreshes and tones all skin types. Like lemon oil, however, it should not be used before going out into sunshine.

FLOWER OILS

The finest of the flower oils are listed below: rose, jasmine and neroli. As they are all quite costly, it may be impractical to buy them all; instead, why not choose your favourite and use it sparingly – a very little goes a long way.

Rose: Good rose oil can be bought in small quantities and is worth the investment for its incomparable fragrance and the fact that its gentle, soothing qualities make it particularly suitable for use in creams and lotions. Scented rose petals can be floated in a bath, or used to add colour and scent to bath salts and skin tonics.

Jasmine: A sensual and fragrant oil that lifts the spirits, jasmine oil is beneficial to older skins. Like rose petals, jasmine flowers can be used to scent a bath.

Neroli: Made from orange blossom, this essential oil is delicately fragrant and is also extensively used in perfumery. It induces a wonderful sense of well-being and relaxation.

Marigold: Although not used as an essential oil, this pretty garden flower's properties are used in creams for healing cuts and grazes (see page 110).

WOOD OILS

As the name suggests, these oils are derived from aromatic woods and have a resinous quality to them that is very attractive. Their fragrance is not overtly feminine and so they are suitable for use in oils and lotions for men as well as women.

Sandalwood: Sandalwood oil is used in skin-care products because it helps balance the production of the natural oils in the skin. It is useful in the treatment of acne and other skin conditions such as excessive oiliness.

Cedarwood: Antiseptic and gently astringent, this oil helps in the treatment of skin conditions. However, it must not be used during pregnancy.

Frankincense: Made from a resin exuded by the bark of a shrubby tree, frankincense oil is excellent for use in creams and lotions for mature skins, and to treat any skin complaint.

Clockwise from top left: Lavender, rosemary, chamomile, marigold, jasmine, rose, orange and lemon. Essential oils are traditionally extracted from herbs, fruit and flowers by one of three methods: distillation, extraction or expression. Although the scale and apparatus have altered over the centuries, the basic methods are the same.

Massage oils and lotions

In the past, the country dweller would have balked at the idea of using massage oils and lotions, considering them far too hedonistic and time-wasting for hard-working folk, yet examination of the medicine cupboard would almost certainly have revealed a selection of liniments and embrocations for rubbing into stiff muscles. The names may have changed, but their purpose remains the same, and if we have now introduced more pleasure into the process, this is no bad thing. Indeed, what could be more pleasurable than a relaxing bath and a massage?

MIXING ESSENTIAL OILS
Make sure all containers are thoroughly cleaned and dry before mixing oils.

Above: *The healing properties of marigolds have been known for centuries and the dried petals can be added to creams and lotions.*

MASSAGE OIL
Massage oils are a mixture of a base oil and aromatic essential oils. With the exception of lavender and tea tree oils, essential oil should never be used undiluted on the skin. When making an oil for use on babies and small children, halve the quantity of essential oil in the recipe. A variety of base oils is available and if you are in any doubt, check for sensitivity with a patch test (see page 76). The vegetable and nut oils used in aromatherapy have been cold-pressed for this purpose, so do not be tempted to substitute ordinary

1 *Pour the base oil into a spotlessly clean and dry container.*

2 *Slowly add drops of essential oil into the container and mix thoroughly.*

cooking oils, which may well have had chemical stabilizers added to them. This recipe includes 10% wheatgerm oil, which improves the keeping qualities of the massage oil and, being high in Vitamin E, makes it particularly good for the skin.

Makes 50ml/3½ tbsp
45ml/3 tbsp almond oil
5ml/1tsp wheatgerm oil
10 drops chamomile oil
  (for relaxation)
  or
10 drops geranium oil
  (for gentle stimulation)

Pour the almond and wheatgerm oils into a clean glass bottle, add the essential oil of your choice and shake to mix. Store in a cool place away from the light.

TEA TREE MASSAGE LOTION

Tea tree is one of the great healing oils, with wonderful antiseptic properties. It has a fresh, resinous smell, which makes it an ideal oil for use in a massage lotion for both men and women.

Makes 150ml/¼ pint/⅔ cup
2.5ml/½ tsp borax
7.5ml/½ tbsp white beeswax
45ml/3 tbsp coconut oil
30ml/2 tbsp almond oil
15ml/1 tbsp wheatgerm oil
20 drops tea tree oil

Dissolve the borax in 60ml/4 tbsp boiled water. Melt the beeswax with the coconut, almond and wheatgerm oils in a double boiler over a gentle heat. Remove from the heat when completely melted and slowly pour in the borax solution, while stirring continuously with a whisk. The lotion will begin to emulsify (turn milky and thicken) immediately.

Continue to whisk until the mixture has cooled, then add the tea tree oil. Pour the lotion into a glass bottle or jar, and preferably one that is coloured. Store the container in a cool place away from direct sunlight.

Above: *Plain glass bottles are ideal containers for storing your soothing massage lotions and oils. Bottles with glass stoppers were once used in pharmacies and copies of these are now readily available.*

LAVENDER BODY LOTION

This creamy lotion is perfect for treating dry skin in winter and can also be used to soothe sunburnt skin, as lavender oil is a very effective treatment for burns.

Makes 120ml/4fl oz/1/2 cup
1.5ml/¼ tsp borax
5ml/1 tsp white beeswax
5ml/1 tsp lanolin
30ml/2 tbsp petroleum jelly
25ml/5 tsp apricot kernel oil
20ml/4 tsp cold-pressed sunflower oil
20 drops lavender oil

1 *Dissolve the borax in 30ml/2 tbsp boiled water. Melt the beeswax, lanolin and petroleum jelly with the apricot kernel and sunflower oil in a double boiler. Remove from the heat once the wax has melted and stir well to blend.*

2 *Add the borax solution, whisking as you do so. The lotion will turn white and thicken but keep whisking until it is cool. Then stir in the lavender oil. Pour into a glass jar or bottle and store in a cool, dark place.*

Above: *Lavender is a popular herb to grow in the garden.*

PEPPERMINT BODY LOTION

This lotion is made as for the lavender body lotion, but using only 10 drops of peppermint oil. Use this refreshing and invigorating lotion after hard physical work. Do not use on small children or during pregnancy.

LAVENDER BUBBLE BATH

There is no need to buy commercially made bubble baths again. This bubble bath is quite delicious and so simple to make that you can prepare some extra as gifts for friends and family.

Makes 1 bottle
a bunch of lavender
1 large bottle clear organic shampoo
5 drops lavender oil

Place the bunch of lavender head down in a clean, wide-necked screw-top jar. You only really need the flowers, so cut off any long stalks. Add the shampoo and lavender oil. Close the jar and place it on a sunny windowsill for two to three weeks, shaking occasionally. Strain the liquid and re-bottle.

HERBAL BATH BAGS

Hang from the bath tap and run hot water through these herbal bags.

Makes 3 bags
three 23cm/9in diameter muslin (cheesecloth) circles
90ml/6 tbsp bran
15ml/1 tbsp lavender flowers
15ml/1 tbsp chamomile flowers
15ml/1 tbsp rosemary tips
3 small rubber bands
3m/3yd narrow ribbon or twine

Place two tablespoons of bran in the centre of each circle of muslin. Add lavender to one, chamomile to a second and rosemary to a third. Gather the material up, close with a rubber band and tie with ribbon.

Right: *Lavender body lotion.*

Bath oils and scrubs

Lying in a bath of fragrant scented oils or exfoliating and nourishing the skin with a scrub are not traditional pastimes for country dwellers. In the past, bathrooms were extremely basic or even non-existent and bathing was for cleanliness rather than pleasure. But now that modern bathrooms are generally warm and comfortable, as well as functional, these activities can be enjoyed and make a pleasurable reward for a hard afternoon's work digging or harvesting in the garden. Of course, big fluffy towels that are fresh from the airing cupboard or linen closet or warmed on a heated bath rail are essential!

LUXURIOUS BODY SCRUB

This is a delightful alternative to the loofah, much more gentle and pleasantly aromatic. After a bath, dry yourself thoroughly and rub the mixture into your skin, paying particular attention to dry skin areas. Leave it to dry on the skin and then rub off using a soft flannel while standing in the bath. It will leave your skin feeling soft and clean. It can be stored in the bathroom in pretty shell containers.

Makes about 150g/5oz
30ml/2 tbsp powdered
* orange rind*
45ml/3 tbsp ground almonds
30ml/2 tbsp oatmeal
15ml/1 tbsp red rose petals
about 90ml/6 tbsp almond oil
5 drops flower oil (jasmine, rose,
* neroli or lavender)*
5 drops wood oil (sandalwood,
* rosewood or cedar)*

1 Blend all the dry ingredients together.

2 Add the almond oil, blending to a crumbly paste. Stir in the essential oils. Store in a glass jar. Use within two weeks.

Above: *Luxurious body scrub.*

ORANGE AND GRAPEFRUIT BATH OIL

At the end of the day, a scented bath is a therapeutic treat. Choose the oils depending on whether you wish to be relaxed or invigorated. An orange and grapefruit bath will gently refresh you. Add one teaspoon to the water only once the bath has been run to avoid the essential oils evaporating before you get in.

Makes 50ml/2fl oz/¼ cup
45ml/3 tbsp sweet almond oil
5 drops grapefruit oil
5 drops orange oil

Combine the oils in a dark-coloured bottle and shake well to combine all the ingredients.

Right: *Orange and grapefruit bath oil and Luxurius body scrub make the daily chore of cleansing your body into an indulgent treat.*

Scented dusting powders

Dusting or talcum powders can be made by blending mica silk, which is a powdered mineral, with cornflour (cornstarch), in a ratio of five to one. Mica silk is often very difficult to find, but a simple solution is to buy unscented talcum powder and blend it with cornflour that you have perfumed with an essential oil of your choice. Rose or jasmine oils are richly perfumed and seductive, while peppermint oil is more sporty and refreshing.

Makes 50g/2oz
75ml/5 tbsp talcum powder
15ml/1 tbsp cornflour
* (cornstarch)*
5 drops rose or jasmine oil
* or 2 drops peppermint oil*

Above: *Use rose essential oil for luxury.*

Above: *Softly seductive rose-scented talc.*

Right: *Talcum powder can be dusted on using a powder puff or from a shaker with a pierced lid.*

Nourishing creams

The countrywoman has always known the value of protecting skin, and these creams provide excellent protection.

TRADITIONAL COLD CREAM

This all-purpose cream can be used to cleanse and soothe the skin.

Makes 200g/7oz
50g/2oz white beeswax
115g/4oz almond oil
2.5ml/½ tsp borax
50ml/2fl oz/¼ cup rosewater

1 *Place the beeswax in a double boiler and add the almond oil. Melt the wax over a gentle heat, stirring all the time.*

2 *Take off the heat and dissolve the borax in the rosewater. Slowly pour it into the melted wax and oil, whisking all the time.*

3 *It will quickly turn milky and thicken. Continue whisking while it cools. When it reaches thick pouring consistency, pour into glass or china pots.*

Above: *Traditional cold cream.*

ROSE-SCENTED MOISTURE CREAM

Rich in nourishing oils and waxes, this moisturizer is a highly effective night cream. If you have difficulty obtaining emulsifying wax, however, use white beeswax instead.

Makes about 175ml/6fl oz/¾ cup
120ml/4fl oz/½ cup rosewater
2.5ml/½ tsp glycerine
30ml/2 tbsp witch hazel
1.5ml/¼ tsp borax
30ml/2 tbsp emulsifying wax or
* white beeswax*
5ml/1 tsp lanolin
30ml/2 tbsp almond oil
2 drops rose oil

Gently heat the rosewater, glycerine, witch hazel and borax in a pan until the borax has dissolved. In a double boiler, melt the wax, lanolin and almond oil over a gentle heat. Slowly add the rosewater mixture to the oil mixture, whisking constantly as you do so. It will quickly turn milky and thicken. Take off the heat, continue to whisk as it cools, and then add the rose oil. Pour the cream into china or glass pots.

UNSCENTED MOISTURE CREAM

Ideal for applying before going outdoors, this simple, unscented cream can be used by both men and women.

Makes about 150ml/¼ pint/⅔ cup
30ml/2 tbsp carnauba wax
15ml/1 tbsp white beeswax
120ml/4fl oz/½ cup almond oil

Melt the waxes and oil in a double boiler over a gentle heat and stir thoroughly to combine. Take off the heat and pour the cream into a container to set.

Right: *Antique pots containing creams.*

Cleansers and skin tonics

Exfoliating washing grains, flower skin tonics and gentle cleansers can be made at home for a fraction of the cost of many commercial products, and if kept in pretty bottles and jars, will look just as attractive on the dressing table.

ALMOND OIL CLEANSER
This gentle cleanser will leave the skin feeling soft and supple.

Makes about 400ml/14fl oz/
1⅔ cups
50g/2oz white beeswax
300ml/½ pint/1¼ cups almond oil
120ml/4fl oz/½ cup rosewater
2.5ml/½ tsp borax
4 drops rose oil (optional)

Melt the beeswax in a double boiler over a gentle heat and slowly add the almond oil. Slightly warm the rosewater and dissolve the borax in it. Pour the rosewater into the oil mixture, whisking all the time as it emulsifies. Take off the heat and keep whisking as it cools. Add the rose oil if required. Pour into glass pots or jars.

ORANGE AND OATMEAL WASHING GRAINS
If you like to wash your face, rather than use cleansers, this is a marvellous once-a-week treatment to exfoliate the skin and leave it feeling soft and glowing. Use the peel of organic oranges because they will not have been sprayed with chemicals or waxes. To use the grains, place a teaspoonful in the palm of the hand, mix to a paste with water and rub gently into the skin; rinse off and dry.

Above: Orange flower and cornflower tonics in pretty glass bottles.

30ml/*2 tbsp fine oatmeal*
15ml/*1 tbsp ground orange peel*

Mix the two ingredients and keep in a lidded bowl or jar in the bathroom.

SKIN TONICS
Different formulations of skin tonics are used to soothe or stimulate the skin. Fine, dry skins need soothing with delicate herbal infusions or flower waters, while large-pored or oily skins benefit from a stimulating tonic containing witch hazel. Skin tonics are made by pouring the ingredients into a glass bottle and shaking. To use, pour a little on to a dampened piece of cotton wool.

Each recipe makes 100ml/6½ tbsp

ORANGE FLOWER SKIN TONIC
(normal skin)
75ml/5 tbsp Orange flower water
25ml/1½ tbsp rosewater

CORNFLOWER SKIN TONIC
(normal skin)
75ml/5 tbsp cornflower infusion
  (see page 110)
25ml/1½ tbsp rosewater

ELDERFLOWER SKIN TONIC
(dry skin)
50ml/3¼ tbsp elderflower infusion
  (see page 76)
50ml/3¼ tbsp rosewater

LAVENDER SKIN TONIC
(oily skin)
75ml/5 tbsp lavender infusion
  (see page 76)
25ml/1½ tbsp witch hazel

LINDEN SKIN TONIC
(for mature skin)
90ml/4¾ tbsp limeflower infusion
  (see page 76)
10ml/1¾ tsp rosewater

Right: *The natural way – simple cosmetics made with pure ingredients. An added bonus, when making your own bathroom treatments, is that you can store them in lovely bottles, jars and pots that make the room look beautiful and match your decor.*

Hand creams and ointments

Richly emollient, these creams and ointments are ideal for hands roughened and sore from gardening and other country tasks. They can also be applied as barrier creams to prevent soreness.

WINTER HAND CREAM
This is a very nourishing cream incorporating patchouli oil, which is a particularly good healer of cracked and chapped skin. Follow the old country treatment for sore hands by covering them in a generous layer of cream last thing at night and then pulling on a pair of soft cotton gloves. Your hands will have absorbed the cream by morning and feel soft once more.

Makes about 475ml/16 fl oz/2 cups
75g/3oz unscented, hard white soap
115g/4oz beeswax
45ml/3 tbsp glycerine
150ml/¼ pint/⅔ cup almond oil
45ml/3 tbsp rosewater
25 drops patchouli oil

Above: *Winter hand cream.*

1 Grate the soap and place it in a bowl. Pour over 90ml/6 tbsp boiling water and stir together until smooth.

2 Combine the beeswax, glycerine, almond oil and rosewater in a double boiler then melt over a gentle heat.

3 Remove from the heat and gradually whisk in the soap mixture. Keep whisking as the mixture cools and thickens. Stir in the patchouli oil and pour into glass or china pots and jars.

Above: *Rose petals.*

HEALING OINTMENT
This is the perfect ointment to use on all the little cuts and scratches that happen while working in the garden. It is also a real barrier against moisture and can be used to protect the hands when working outside in wet weather.

Makes 100ml/6½ tbsp
90ml/6 tbsp white petroleum jelly
2.5ml/½ tsp paraffin wax
1.5ml/¼ tsp anhydrous lanolin
10 drops essential oil (lemon, tea tree or lavender)

Place the petroleum jelly, paraffin wax and lanolin in a double boiler and melt slowly over a gentle heat, stirring constantly. Once melted, remove the boiler from the heat and continue stirring the mixture as it cools and thickens. Stir in the essential oil and store in a china or dark glass container.

Right: *Hard-working hands will benefit from regular skin care.*

Hair rinses and treatments

Both fresh herbs and essential oils can be used to promote hair and scalp health. Many of the hair products used today leave a residue that can dull the hair and affect the condition of the scalp. Regular use of a herbal hair rinse and an occasional oil treatment will restore shine and stimulate the scalp.

CIDER VINEGAR HAIR RINSE
This is a traditional country beauty treatment to invigorate the scalp and give the hair a deep shine. Use as a final rinse for the hair, towel dry, gently comb through and leave to dry naturally.

Makes 1.2 litres/2 pints/5 cups
250ml/8fl oz/1 cup cider vinegar

Mix the cider vinegar with 1 litre/ 1¾ pints/4 cups warm water and use as the final hair rinse.

CHAMOMILE HAIR RINSE
This can be used by people with fair hair and also children. Use in the same way as the rosemary hair rinse (below). If left in the hair, it is supposed to lighten the hair colour, especially when dried in the sun, but avoid prolonged exposure to the sun as this can make the hair dry.

Makes 1 litre/1¾ pints/4 cups
50g/2oz chamomile flowers
150ml/¼ pint/⅔ cup cider vinegar
5 drops chamomile oil

Make this rinse in the same way as the rosemary hair rinse.

Above: *Store your hair rinses and oils in pretty bottles alongside decorative sea shells.*

ROSEMARY HAIR RINSE
Rosemary is a marvellous and effective hair conditioner, especially for dark hair. With the addition of some rosemary essential oil, this rinse is a natural treatment for dandruff and other related scalp conditions. You should use it once a week to promote and improve the health of your hair. Do not use if you are pregnant or suspect that you might be pregnant.

Makes 1.2 litres/2 pints/5 cups
50g/2oz sprigs of rosemary
300ml/½ pint/1¼ cups cider vinegar
10 drops rosemary oil

Pour 900ml/1½ pints/3¾ cups boiling water over the rosemary sprigs, cover and leave to infuse overnight. Strain the liquid through muslin (cheesecloth), add the vinegar and the essential oil, then pour into a stoppered bottle.

OIL TREATMENT FOR HAIR

Hair that is regularly exposed to the elements can become dry. An oil treatment once a month will work wonders for your hair and scalp. Apply a small amount to to coat the hair rather than saturate it, and gently massage it in with your fingers. Cover with a hot towel and leave for 20 minutes, then shampoo off and rinse thoroughly.

Above: *Herbal treatments restore shine to your hair and can help to improve scalp conditions.*

Makes 4–6 treatments
90ml/6 tbsp coconut oil
3 drops rosemary oil
2 drops tea tree oil
2 drops lavender oil

Blend the oils and store in dark-coloured bottles.

The Still Room

Tempting ideas for scenting and decorating your home, along with natural remedies and recipes from the still room.

The history of the still room

In Tudor times, in the 16th century, the still room could be described as the control centre of the domestic economy. It was here that the countrywoman would store her precious herbs and spices, and make lotions, potions and distillations. In doing so, she could be described as the family doctor, pharmacist, herbalist, perfumer, candlemaker and pest controller all rolled into one, and the health and well-being of everyone in the household was her responsibility.

Her knowledge was of a very practical nature, based on skill, observation and recipes passed from generation to generation. Her day, her week, her year were full of myriad tasks which had to be completed to keep her home running efficiently, and it is not surprising that few had the time, energy or learning to write down their recipes and formulae. From the manuscripts that do survive, it is clear that these women were full of common sense and a real understanding of the materials they worked with, apparently in marked contrast to the herbalists and doctors of the time who were much inclined to invoke magical powers and use disgusting and dangerous ingredients in their cures.

Nowadays, potpourri, flower waters and scented candles are pleasing and decorative accessories, but in the Tudor household they were essential to ward off dreadful odours and keep pests and disease at bay. Indeed, the scents they used were far from subtle.

Herbs were gathered, dried, stored and used in large quantities to add savour to food and disguise the less than fresh taste of most meat as well as for numerous medicinal infusions, distillations and for strewing underfoot.

Spices were precious commodities, carefully guarded by the housewife who would keep them under lock and key and closely supervise their use. Although expensive, they were used in huge amounts: we would find these quantities quite overpowering, but like herbs, they were a disguise for rancid flavours. Their curative powers were also well recognized and respected.

The modern still room projects are, in many ways, highly romanticized versions of their medieval equivalents. We make these things for pleasure rather than for practical purposes, nevertheless they are fragrant, decorative and sometimes functional. By passing on these methods, we help to continue a tradition that has been an essential part of country life for centuries.

Left: *Fragrant and colourful dried flowers are stored in glass jars ready to be blended with herbs, spices and fixatives to make aromatic potpourris which can be used throughout the home.*

Above: *If you want to use roses in potpourris, gather them before their petals drop. Spread the petals on absorbent paper to dry, then pack them in airtight jars or boxes.*

Right: *Aromatic herbs and spices have always been highly prized. In the past, wars were fought for control of the spice routes and the spice merchants were often men of almost limitless wealth.*

Potpourris

There are three elements to a potpourri: the fragrance, the fixatives and the filler. The fragrance comes from a blend of oils and spices; the fixatives keep the fragrance from evaporating; and the filler is the flower petals, leaves, cones and other materials that make up the potpourri. Once mixed, 'cure' the ingredients in a sealed container for six weeks so that the fragrance is fixed in the filler and loses its initial raw edge.

Essential oils, whole and ground spices and fixatives can be bought from herbalists and specialist suppliers. The fixatives used in these recipes are orris, which is the powdered root of *Iris florentina*, and gum benzoin (gum benjamin), which is a resin from the styrax tree. The recipes here are for dry potpourris because wet potpourris are more time-consuming to make and smell a lot better than they look.

Do not place your potpourri in bright light or the flowers will quickly fade. Stir it to release its fragrance, and to revive it, return the potpourri to the curing pan with a new spice and oil blend or, for a quick fix, sprinkle on a few drops of brandy.

WARNING: Certain essential oils should not be handled by pregnant women or anyone who may be pregnant or where there is an existing medical condition. Some oils can irritate sensitive skin and it is therefore advisable to wear rubber gloves when handling the concentrated oil and spice blends.

SUMMER POTPOURRI

Gather a few flowers each time you go out and place them on a wire rack in a warm place to dry. Pick rose petals from full-blown roses, spread them out to dry and use them as the base for the potpourri.

15ml/1 tbsp ground cinnamon
15ml/1 tbsp ground orris root
1 whole nutmeg, grated
40 drops lavender oil
40 drops rose geranium oil
10 drops mandarin oil
1.75 litres/3 pints/7½ cups dried
 flower petals and heads (rose petals,
 rosebuds, peonies, lavender,
 pink peppercorns)

Mix together the cinnamon, orris and nutmeg in a mortar. Add the essential oils and blend to a moist powder using the pestle. Measure the flower petals into a large mixing bowl and mix thoroughly with the oil and spice mixture. Place the potpourri mixture in a large, lidded ceramic or glass container and leave to cure for six weeks, stirring it occasionally. The potpourri is then ready for use.

Above: *Summer potpourri.*

Above: *Spice Islands potpourri.*

SPICE ISLANDS POTPOURRI

An exotic blend of nuts, pods, spices and chillies with spice and wood oils. This chunky potpourri looks good displayed in a wooden or earthenware bowl. You can use the nuts that did not get eaten at Christmas in the filler and take the opportunity to replace any whole spices that have been in the cupboard too long.

10ml/2 tsp ground anise
5ml/1 tsp ground nutmeg
5ml/1 tsp ground cinnamon
5ml/1 tsp allspice powder
5ml/1 tsp ground cloves
10ml/2 tsp gum benzoin
 (gum benjamin)
25 drops cinnamon oil
10 drops ginger oil
10 drops orange oil
10 drops patchouli oil
5 drops sandalwood or vetiver oil
1.75 litres/3 pints/7½ cups dried filler
 ingredients (whole star anise, brazil
 nuts, chillies, cinnamon sticks, whole
 nutmegs and bakuli pods)

Mix all the spices and the gum
benzoin in a mortar. Blend in the oils
with a pestle to make a moist powder.
Measure the filler ingredients into a
large bowl and add the oil and spice
mixture. Place the potpourri in a
lidded ceramic or glass container and
leave to cure for six weeks, stirring or
shaking occasionally. It is then ready
to display in a shallow bowl.

AUTUMN POTPOURRI

The subtle, mellow colours of
autumn are captured in this attractive potpourri with its orange and
green Chinese lanterns mixed with
oak leaves, acorns and cones. An
unusual blend of spices and
oils gives the mixture a clean,
tangy fragrance.

15ml/1 tbsp freshly ground coarse
  black pepper
15ml/1 tbsp freshly ground coriander
5ml/1 tsp ground ginger
30ml/2 tbsp gum benzoin
  (gum benjamin)
20 drops ginger oil
20 drops lime oil
5 drops basil oil
5 drops juniper oil
1.75 litres/3 pints/7½ cups dried filler
  ingredients (Chinese lanterns, Physalis,
  oak leaves, acorns, seed heads, small
  cones and golden mushrooms)

Mix the spices and the gum benzoin
together in a mortar. Use a pestle to
blend in the oils to make a powder,
then measure the filler ingredients
into a large bowl and blend with the
powder. Place the mixture in a large,
lidded ceramic or glass container and
leave it to cure for about six weeks,
stirring or shaking occasionally. The
potpourri is then ready for use.

Right: *Clockwise from top left;*
Autumn potpourri, Spice Islands pot-
pourri, and Summer potpourri.

Room fresheners and burners

Once you have a range of essential oils, you can easily perfume your house. Fragrance influences mood, and by using a refreshing oil like lemon or grapefruit, you can stimulate a feeling of energy and concentration, while a sensual oil like jasmine will create a romantic mood.

SPRAYER
You can dilute an essential oil at the ratio of 10 drops of oil to 105ml/ 7 tbsp of water and use it in a sprayer. If possible, use a metal or ceramic sprayer as the oils will deteriorate if stored in plastic.

VAPORIZER
The traditional vaporizer consists of a pierced ceramic bowl which holds a night-light or candle over which is placed a small saucer of essential oil diluted with water. As the water is warmed, the oil is diffused into the air. Use a vaporizer at Christmas to create an instant atmosphere by warming a mixture of cinnamon and orange oils.

CERAMIC RING
This is porous to absorb oil and fits over a light bulb. As the ring is warmed, the fragrance is diffused. There have been reports of these exploding (though I have never had any problems), so check on their safety.

DRIED ORANGES
Oranges, particularly Seville oranges, are fragrant when dried. Place some in a bowl to scent a room. When their fragrance begins to fade, you can rejuvenate them with bergamot or sweet orange oil.

Above: *Richly fragrant and attractive dried Seville oranges.*

Make a series of vertical cuts through the skin of each orange. Place the oranges on a wire rack in a baking tray and leave overnight in a very low oven with the door slightly ajar (the oranges give off a great deal of moisture, which needs to evaporate). Put the rack in a warm place like an airing cupboard or linen closet, and leave to dry for at least a week, until the oranges feel hard and light.

POMANDERS
Pomanders have been popular since Tudor times because their fragrance is delicious and long-lasting. A well-made pomander will still give off its scent years later. Seville oranges are the finest for this purpose (select only unblemished ones; the cloves should also be the best). Hang pomanders in wardrobes and cupboards.

Makes 6 pomanders
115g/4oz ground cinnamon
50g/2oz ground cloves
15g/½oz ground allspice
15g/½oz freshly grated nutmeg
15g/½oz ground coriander
25g/1oz ground orris root
6 Seville oranges
115g/4oz whole cloves

Mix all the ground spices and orris root in a lidded earthenware dish large enough to hold all the oranges. Stud the oranges with cloves, using a cocktail stick (toothpick) or large needle to make the holes. Roll the oranges in the spice mixture and leave them in the spices to cure. Cover the dish and stand in a warm place for at least four weeks. Turn the pomanders daily. If the spice mix feels damp, leave the lid at an angle to allow the moisture to evaporate. After four weeks the oranges will have shrunk and hardened and the pomanders will be ready to use.

DOOR SACHETS
This is an easy way to scent a room. Make small fabric bags (see page 106) and fill them with potpourri or cotton wool impregnated with essential oil (ensure that the oil is at the centre of the cotton wool or it may stain the fabric). Fasten the sachets with ribbon or cord and hang them on door handles. As the door is opened and closed it will waft the fragrance around the room.

Right: *Fill your home with fragrances which blend into a tapestry of natural, subtle scents.*

Scented sachets and bags

Like potpourri, sachets and bags can be used to scent your home. Use them in drawers and cupboards, tucked in among cushions on the sofa and under your pillow.

LAVENDER BAGS
The most traditional of all sweet bags, the lavender bag has enjoyed such enduring popularity because it is deliciously fragrant and keeps moths at bay.

Makes 5 bags
30 x 120cm/12 x 48in fabric
needle and thread
dressmaker's pins
1.25m/1½yd ribbon or cord (optional)
For the filling:
75g/3oz lavender
25g/1oz ground orris root
25 drops lavender oil

1 *Cut the fabric into two pieces across the width. One should be 25 x 120cm/ 10 x 48in, and the other 5 x 120cm/ 2 x 48in. Cut each piece of fabric into five equal pieces. The larger pieces will make the bags and the smaller pieces will make the ties. Turn in a 5cm/2in seam allowance on one edge of each bag and hem.*

2 *Fold in half, right sides together, and pin along the unhemmed edges. Stitch along the pin line. Turn the right way out; press. To make ties, fold the smaller pieces of fabric in half lengthways, pin and stitch along the side and one end. Turn the right way out. Fold in and stitch the unfinished end, then press.*

3 *Divide the filling between the bags and fasten each bag with a tie. Or, fasten each bag with a 25cm/10in piece of ribbon or cord.*

Left: *The ever-popular lavender bag.*

Right: *Use remnants and scraps for bags.*

ROSE AND LAVENDER-SCENTED CUSHION

Scented cushions are a charming way to fragrance the home. They release their aroma every time they are leaned against. The fragrance will last well, but make the cushion cover removable so that you can replace the mixture.

50g/2oz rose petals and buds
10g/¼oz lavender flowers
10g/¼oz oakmoss (optional)
5 bay leaves, crumbled
15ml/1 tbsp ground cinnamon
15ml/1 tbsp ground orris root
10 drops rose oil
40cm/16in square piece of muslin (cheesecloth)
needle and thread
50cm/20in square piece of thick wadding (batting)
50cm/20in square cushion cover

1 *Mix all the dry ingredients in a bowl and add the rose oil.*

2 *Fold the muslin in half twice and seam along two sides to create a bag 20cm/8in square. Fill with the mixture and stitch the opening closed.*

3 *Place the scented bag on the wadding and fold the wadding over the bag. Stitch around the wadding to create the pad for the cushion. Slip the scented cushion pad into the cover.*

ROSE-SCENTED SACHETS

Make these wonderfully fragrant sachets in exactly the same way as the lavender bags on page 106, and then fill them with the following:

75g/3oz scented red rose petals
25g/1oz ground orris root
25 drops rose oil

Above: *Scented sachets are a simple, yet delightful gift to receive.*

MOTH-REPELLENT SACHETS

These miniature cushions are stuffed with herbs that repel moths. They can be tucked in among your clothes to protect them from attack. Use equal quantities of southernwood (*Artemisia abrotanum*), tansy (*Tanacetum vulgare*) and santolina.

PEPPERMINT SACHETS

Sachets or bags filled with peppermints may help to alleviate nausea. An excellent use for these sachets is to carry them in the car or on a plane as a comfort for children or adults who suffer from travel sickness.

Right: *A scented cushion tucked in among the others on a sofa will release its delicate fragrance when it is leaned against.*

Natural remedies and medicines

In the past, the ability to treat family coughs and colds, cuts and scratches was of vital importance to the country housewife, and she would pride herself on her knowledge and the array of lotions, ointments and infusions she kept in her still-room. Most of the plants and herbs used then still grow wild in some of our fields and hedgerows, but few of us have the time and certainly not the knowledge to concoct the numerous cures and treatments that made up her pharmacy. Nevertheless, there are some old-fashioned remedies that we can still easily and safely use.

Honey and lemon is a tried and trusted remedy for most sore throats. To make it, mix the juice of a large lemon with 15ml/1 tbsp of clear honey (or more, according to taste) and dilute with boiling water to make a wonderfully soothing hot drink.

Peppermint tea is a safe and palatable cure for indigestion and nausea.

Chamomile tea will calm restless children and help ensure a good night's sleep for children and grown-ups alike.

Sage and honey tea is a comforting treatment for colds, coughs and sore throats. Add 15g/½oz sage leaves to 15ml/1 tbsp clear honey and the juice of a lemon, then dilute with 300ml/½ pint/1¼ cups boiling water. Cover and leave to infuse for about 20–30 minutes. Strain and serve hot.

Calendula (marigold) cream is still popular as a treatment for cuts and scratches. To obtain an extract of marigold, tightly pack the flower heads into a wide-necked jar, close and leave on a sunny windowsill for seven to ten days. Strain off the oily

sediment that forms at the bottom of the bottle. Substitute this extract for the essential oil in the healing ointment recipe (see page 94). Apply the cream to minor cuts and sores.

Witch hazel dabbed on to bites and stings will relieve the pain.

Cornflower infusion soothes tired and sore eyes. Infuse 30ml/2 tbsp cornflower flowers in 120ml/4fl oz/½ cup water. Cover and leave to cool. Strain and soak cotton wool pads with the infusion. Leave on the eyelids for 15 minutes.

Garlic is a powerful, if somewhat smelly, antiseptic. Taken regularly in food it is thought to purify the blood and lower cholesterol.

Rosehip and hibiscus tea is a rich source of vitamin C and will help keep coughs and colds at bay.

Elderflower and peppermint tea taken early will relieve feverishness.

Rosewater or orange flower water added in very small amounts to hot water can be drunk daily to keep the skin clear and soothe the digestion. Only culinary-quality flower waters should be used in this way.

Left: *Healing herbs and flowers kept in the compartments of an old stone dish.*

Right: *Simple home remedies can be used to help treat minor complaints such as a cold.*

Scented polishes

Old-fashioned polishes are coming back into favour as we discover that spray polishes seldom give furniture the deep, glowing shine of a natural wax polish.

BEESWAX AND TURPENTINE POLISH

This is a very simple polish to make and the addition of wood oils will give it an attractive resinous fragrance. Lemon or lavender essential oil may also be used in this polish. Apply the polish to your furniture using a soft cloth, leave a few minutes to dry, then buff vigorously with a soft duster to achieve a deep, lustrous shine.

Makes 250ml/8fl oz/1 cup
75g/3oz natural beeswax
200ml/7fl oz/¾ cup pure turpentine
20 drops cedarwood oil
10 drops sandalwood oil

Above: *Beeswax and linseed oil.*

1 *Grate the beeswax coarsely and place in a screw-top jar.*

2 *Pour on the turpentine, screw on the lid and leave for a week, stirring occasionally until the mixture becomes a smooth cream. Add the essential oils and mix them in well. The polish is then ready to use.*

FURNITURE REVIVER

Wooden surfaces can become grimy from a combination of dirt and a build-up of spray polish. Use this traditional country recipe to loosen the grime and feed the wood at the same time. It works best if it is used over a few weeks, as it will gradually remove the layers of polish and, once the surface is cleaned, you can return to a conventional furniture polish.

Apply with a soft cloth, leave for a few minutes, then wipe off with a second cloth.

Makes 750ml/1¼ pints/3 cups
250ml/8fl oz/1 cup malt vinegar
250ml/8fl oz/1 cup pure turpentine
250ml/8fl oz/1 cup raw linseed oil
15ml/1 tbsp granulated (white) sugar

Measure all the ingredients into a bottle with a cork or screw top, seal and shake to mix. Label the bottle clearly.

CLEANING VINEGARS

Malt vinegar is an extremely versatile and effective household cleaner, especially in areas where limescale from hard water is a problem. At its simplest, vinegar can be used undiluted to give a brilliant clarity to newly cleaned windows. Wipe over the window with a cloth or sponge dipped in vinegar and then polish dry with a crumpled piece of newspaper – this is an old but reliable way of achieving sparkling windows. Similarly, keep a spray bottle of vinegar in the

Above: A selection of traditional cloths, brushes and polishes stands ready for spring cleaning treasured pieces of furniture.

bathroom and use it to keep shower screens free of water marks and prevent the build up of limescale on tiles, baths and basins.

113

Rolled beeswax candles

Candles made from sheets of beeswax are very easy to make, beautiful to look at and aromatic to burn. Good-quality beeswax retains a strong scent of honey and the sweet smell will fill the room when the candles are lit. The wax should be at room temperature before rolling, otherwise it may be difficult to work with. A hairdryer set at a low temperature will help soften the wax without melting it.

Makes one candle
23cm/9in length of wick
20 x 35cm/8 x 13¾in sheet of beeswax
melted beeswax for brushing
paintbrush

Above: *A fragrant beeswax candle.*

1 *Lay the wick across the width of the beeswax sheet and cut it so that it is slightly longer than the sheet. The protruding end will be used for lighting.*

2 *Gently fold the wax over the wick and roll the sheet into a cylinder.*

3 *Prime the protruding wick by brushing it with melted wax.*

SCENTED CANDLES

Candles that look beautiful and smell wonderful are my favourite way of scenting a room. When making them, essential oils can be used singly or combined to create the fragrance of your choice. Old terracotta pots make simple but good-looking moulds for the candles and can be used again and again. Scent with flower oils for a candlelit dinner, citronella or rosemary to keep insects at bay on a summer's evening and frankincense for festivals.

Fills one 10cm/4in container
a small piece of putty or clay
115g/4oz paraffin wax
25g/1oz beeswax
15cm/6in of 18mm/¾in wick
25 drops essential oil

Block the hole in the base of the container with the putty or clay. Melt the paraffin and beeswax together in a double boiler over a gentle heat. Add the essential oil.

Dip the wick into the melted wax, then push the end of the wick into the clay or putty and position it centrally in the container. Pour the melted wax into the container. Drape the end of the wick over a spoon handle or stick laid on the rim of the container to hold it in its central position while the wax sets. As the wax cools, a dip will form around the wick. Fill this with more wax if you wish.

Right: *The soft glow of candlelight is flattering and relaxing, and if you have a stock of candles, you can easily create a mysterious and romantic ambience.*

Garlands and swags

As the seasons change, so do the flowers and natural decorations in the country home: the daffodils and bluebells of spring; the cow parsley and dog-roses of summer; and the brightly coloured berries and leaves of autumn. Other natural decorations also make their way indoors: autumn leaves gathered while walking down the lane and brought indoors as treasures, an abandoned bird's nest found in a winter hedgerow or a basket of pine cones picked in the woods.

A MOSS AND TWIG GARLAND

Mosses and lichens are the main materials for this garland, with twigs, cones and golden mushrooms adding the finishing touches. I pick up attractive fallen twigs and cones regularly when I am out for walks but I buy all the other materials from good dried flower suppliers, and so should you unless you have a plentiful supply available on your own land. When working with carpet moss it should be torn rather than cut to ensure that pieces join up in a natural-looking way.

florist's wire
30cm/12in straw ring
selection of mosses such as carpet
 moss, oakmoss, spanish moss,
 reindeer moss and bun moss,
 all used here
German pins or pins made from
 bent florist's wire
glue gun and glue sticks
small cones
golden mushrooms
twigs

1 Attach a loop of wire to the back of the wreath. Cover the ring with carpet moss, pinning it as you go, until covered. Start to position and pin the other mosses.

2 Alternatively, glue the mosses in place. Add the cones, mushrooms and twigs.

3 Fasten the cones together by twisting a piece of wire in between the layers of scales at the base of each cone. Apply some glue to the base of the cones before pinning them in place.

4 Glue the mushrooms in position and use pins to fasten small groups of twigs to the garland.

A HERB GARLAND

A length of twiggy vine that has been twisted into a circle and tied in shape makes the base of this garland. Bunches of herbs are then tied to the ring with string to allow the herbs to be removed for use in cooking. Remember though that herbs exposed to direct sunlight and dust will not be as aromatic and tasty as those that have been stored in sealed jars in the store cupboard or pantry.

Above: *A herb garland.*
Right: *A garland of moss, twigs and cones.*

Above: *A spicy garland.*

A BAY LEAF RING

This is a lovely way to store your bay leaves. The ring below makes a simple decoration and the bay leaves are always readily to hand. The fresh leaves are threaded on to plastic-coated garden wire which is twisted into a circle and decorated with a raffia bow.

Above: *A bay leaf ring.*

A SPICY GARLAND

To make this colourful and flavourful garland, galvanized wire is shaped into a circle (coat hanger wire is ideal) and the chillies and orange rind are threaded on. The chillies and orange rind can be broken off to use in cooking or the garland can be treated purely as a decorative object.

A HOP AND HYDRANGEA SWAG

In the autumn the hop bines are harvested for use in the brewing industry. They dry most attractively and can also be used to make natural swags to decorate beams or the tops of

cupboards and dressers. During the year their colour will fade, so that by the following autumn, you will be ready to take them down and replace them with the new season's hops. Hop bines are quite brittle so it is advisable to spray them with water and leave them overnight before you work with them. They can be pinned in place or tied to sisal rope as they have been for this swag, which has been decorated with bunches of hydrangeas tied on with hessian bows. Poppy seedheads, pink rosebuds and pink peppercorns add a touch of colour.

Right: *A hop bine decorated with roses, hydrangeas, berries and poppy seedheads.*

Basket of dried flowers

The summer garden is full of richly coloured flowers, many of which can be dried. Even flowers such as buttercups, cornflowers and love-in-the-mist can be dried by hanging them upside down in an airy place. A jug or pitcher of these on a dresser will bring back memories of summer long after it has passed, while a basket of dried flowers is a constant reminder of the garden.

The secret of successful dried flower arranging is to build the outline of the arrangement out of florist's foam and then cut the flower stems short, so that you can pack the flowers in tightly next to one another and control the shape that you are creating. It is also important not to fill the basket entirely with star performers such as peonies and roses, partly because this would make the arrangement expensive, but also because they create far more impact scattered among simpler flowers or greenery. Display dried flowers out of the sun and blow over them with a cold hairdryer every now and then to keep them free of dust and insects. Dried flowers should be renewed annually.

rustic basket, about
    18 x 23cm/7 x 9in
2 blocks dry florist's foam
2 pieces florist's wire
glue gun and glue
    sticks (optional)
2 bunches pale yellow achillea
1 bunch pink achillea
2 bunches carthamnus
6 pale pink peonies
3 cerise peonies
12 cerise roses

1 *Cut one of the blocks of florist's foam so that it fills the basket and then build a second layer with the other block. Pin the foam together with long pins made from the florist's wire or glue them using a glue gun.*

2 *Starting at one side of the basket begin to build the arrangement with groups of one type of flower or greenery interspersed with the occasional peony or group of roses.*

Step back regularly as you work to check that the arrangement is taking on a balanced shape. Bear in mind that the flowers may be viewed from a low angle and crouch down to check that there are no gaps that need filling around the edge of the basket.

Above: *Mass the flowers for a full effect.*

A TERRACOTTA POT OF FLOWERS

An old terracotta pot is a sympathetic container for a small group of dried flowers. An arrangement such as this is perfect for a bedside table in a guest room or as a gift to remind a friend of your summer garden. As with the basket (above) the shape of the arrangement is built out of foam, which is cut into a dome shape above the edge of the pot. Some very short-

Above: *Dried flowers in a terracotta pot.*

Above: *An arrangement should feature groups of flowers to create distinct blocks of colour.*

stemmed flowers are then pushed into position. To ensure the flowers stay in place, it is advisable to use a glue gun to apply a little glue to their base. For this arrangement, carpet moss has been tucked under the flowers and glued to the pot to complete the natural effect.

Natural decorations and treats

BIRD NUT BALL

In later autumn and the winter months, the birds in the garden will appreciate extra food to help them through the cold weather and we will enjoy the sight of them regularly visiting the bird table. Take the opportunity to clear out your store cupboard or pantry and replace any stale nuts and dried fruits before you start preparing for Christmas in earnest.

equal quantities of melted fat
  and breadcrumbs
nuts, seeds and dried fruit
string
dried apricots
peanuts in their shells

Mix together the melted fat and breadcrumbs and stir in half of the nuts, seeds and dried fruit. As the mixture starts to solidify, shape it into a ball around a length of string and place in the refrigerator to harden. Place the remainder of the fruit, seeds and nuts on a piece of newspaper and roll the hardened ball around on it until it is completely covered with the mixture. Make a loop from the string

Above: *Autumnal nuts.*

that protrudes from one side of the ball and thread apricots and peanuts in their shells on to the string on the other side of the ball. Hang the bird treat from your bird table or the branch of a tree.

FRUITY TREE

Glycerined leaves make a perfect foundation for any dried topiary. You can buy them in branches, ready-glycerined for use, or glycerine your own garden prunings. Here they have been wired into bunches for a fabulous, full look.

secateurs (pruners)
3 branches glycerined
  beech leaves
florist's stub wires
dried pear slices

Above: *A fruity tree.*

florist's foam ball, about 13cm/5in
  in diameter
flowerpot, 18cm/7in tall

Cut the leaves off the branches and trim the stalks short. Wire up small bunches of four or six beech leaves and twist the ends of the wires together. Pass a stub wire through the top of each pear slice and twist the ends together. Completely cover the portion of the ball that will show above the pot with beech leaves. Add the pear slices and put the ball into the pot.

Right: *Create a bird nut ball and give the birds in your garden a winter treat.*

Seasonal
Celebrations

Ideas and inspirations for recipes and decorations to
enhance country festivities throughout the year.

The passing seasons

In the countryside the passing of the year has always been marked with festivals and celebrations. From earliest times, when these rites were ceremonies of invocation and offerings to the gods – to ensure that the sun returned after the long winter, that the rain fell in spring and that the harvest was bounteous and safely gathered in – the country dweller has remained in close touch with the seasons, aware that each month brings its allotted tasks and that time must be used wisely and well if all is to be completed.

The major festivals we celebrate today are a mixture of those early pagan rites and celebrations with Christian religious ceremony, brought about when the priests, realising they could not suppress the old ways, decided to incorporate elements of the old festivals into the Catholic Christian festivals.

However we decide to mark these festivals, whether in a religious or secular manner, there is a deeply instinctive need to acknowledge and celebrate seasonal changes. Few of us are untouched by the arrival of spring, the extraordinary emergence of new life from what seems a cold, unwelcoming environment. Within weeks, what was bare brown earth is a carpet of colour as young plants race into lush growth and flower with almost indecent haste. No wonder the priests looked for a serious ceremony to put the lid on all this rising sap and rampant reproduction. In Christianity the weeks leading up to Easter are intended as a time of self-denial and

Above: *Summer celebrations are marked by outdoor meals deliciously flavoured with intensely aromatic fresh herbs, which grow prolifically in this season of warm abundance.*

reflection, but the culmination is a glorious celebration of resurrection and what more appropriate time than spring when the evidence of returning life is all around.

Nowadays, few of us celebrate May Day or Midsummer's Day as would have been done by country people in the past. Instead, we save the summer months for more personal celebrations such as family christenings, weddings or that institution unknown to our forebears, the annual family summer holiday.

The coming of autumn or fall brings the Harvest Festival, which in the country has real meaning and significance. There is a great feeling of relief and achievement when the last of the corn is harvested, when hay and straw are baled and stacked and the crops are lifted. Even the city dweller cannot fail to notice that the market stalls and supermarket shelves are a rich kaleidoscope of sun-ripened produce and the most urban of schools will use this festival as an opportunity to introduce children to the circle of the seasons. In North America, Thanksgiving Day has its origins in harvest festivals, but is now celebrated separately as a national day of thanksgiving and is a time when

Left: *The first spring flowers mean that life is returning to the country. With their vibrant colours and heady aromas, they herald the return of sunshine and blue skies after the long, dark winter.*

far-flung families make an effort to come together, renew ties and share a celebratory meal that makes the most of the season's bounty.

Halloween is the one festival still celebrated today that is predominantly pagan. Its origins are druidic and, though it was given Christian status as All Saints Night, it is generally thought of as the night when the dead return as ghosts to make mischief. Its mix of fear and fun is irresistible to children.

The onset of winter, with its short days and long nights, would be a difficult time to endure if it were not for the anticipation of Christmas. At the darkest time of year, we celebrate a festival of blazing fires, good cheer, good food and good company. For country people it is a time when good husbandry in the earlier months allows time for socializing and relaxing, a welcome break from the hard work of every day, when each of us celebrates in our own way the passing of the old year and the coming of the new.

Above: *The pears, crab apples and other fruit that are harvested in the autumn and stored in the cupboard or pantry hold deep within them the delicious flavour and glowing colour of summer sunshine.*

Right: *The evocative and powerfully resinous scent of pine branches and fir cones slowly spreads through the house as preparations are underway for the coming Christmas festivities.*

Easter

Easter eggs and the Easter rabbit are pre-Christian symbols of fertility that have survived into the festival today. In some areas, the tradition of rolling dyed eggs down a hill persists and it is variously attributed as symbolizing the returning sun or rolling away the stone from Christ's tomb.

SIMNEL CAKE

Halfway through Lent, it was the custom to make a simnel cake, which would be brought out to celebrate Easter Day and the end of the lenten fast. I cannot say that I remember fasting during Lent, but we did enjoy my mother's simnel cake, which was part of our Easter celebrations, along with those other traditional Easter treats, hot cross buns.

Serves 8–12
225g/8oz/2 cups plain
(all-purpose) flour
a pinch of salt
115g/4oz/⅔ cup sultanas
(golden raisins)
50g/2oz chopped almonds
50g/2oz chopped walnuts
40g/1½oz/⅓ cup candied peel
grated rind of half a lemon
75g/3oz crystallized ginger, chopped
175g/6oz/¾ cup glacé (candied)
cherries, quartered
200g/7oz/scant 1 cup butter
175g/6oz/generous ¾ cup caster
(superfine) sugar
4 eggs
5ml/1 tsp vanilla extract
30ml/2 tbsp brandy
apricot jam, sieved, for brushing
500g/1lb 2oz marzipan
food dye, for colouring (optional)

Above: *Simnel cake.*

Preheat the oven to 160°C/325°F/ Gas 3. Sift the flour and salt together into a bowl. Add the sultanas, nuts, candied peel, lemon rind, ginger and cherries and mix until everything is coated with the flour.

Cream the butter with the sugar until soft. Beat in the eggs one at a time, then add the vanilla extract. Gradually stir in the flour and fruit mixture, adding the brandy with the last of the flour. Pour into a lined 20cm/8in diameter cake tin (pan) and bake for 1 hour, then for another hour at 150°C/300°F/Gas 2.

Allow the cake to cool before storing it in an airtight cake tin for four to six days before decorating. Brush over the cake with sieved apricot jam, then roll out the marzipan and cut it to fit the cake. Carefully lay the marzipan over the cake so that it is smooth. Decorate the edge of the cake with a marzipan plait (braid) and the centre with marzipan eggs coloured with a little food dye.

Right: *A feast for Easter day.*

HOT CROSS BUNS

These will be more fragrant if you use freshly ground mixed sweet spices (see page 46).

Makes 20–24
250g/9oz/2¼ cups strong white
  bread flour
250g/9oz/2¼ cups wholemeal
  (whole-wheat) flour
5ml/1 tsp salt
10ml/2 tsp mixed sweet spices
50g/2oz/¼ cup butter
15g/½oz dried yeast
50g/2oz/4 tbsp soft light brown sugar
275ml/9fl oz/1¼ cups warm milk
2 eggs, beaten
115g/4oz/⅔ cup currants
leftover pastry, for the crosses
For the glaze:
30ml/2 tbsp milk
30ml/2 tbsp caster (superfine) sugar

Sift both flours, salt and spices together and rub in the butter. Activate the yeast with 5ml/1 tsp of the sugar and a little of the milk. Make a well in the flour and pour in the yeast mixture, the eggs and the rest of the milk. Mix by hand to a stiffish dough. Add the currants. Cover and leave to rise for about 2 hours until doubled in volume. Knock back (punch down) the dough, knead briefly, divide into 20–24 buns and place on a greased and floured baking tray. Cover and leave to rise until doubled in size. Preheat the oven to 190°C/375°F/Gas 5. Top each with a pastry cross, moistened to stick to the dough. Bake for 15–20 minutes. To make the glaze, boil the milk and sugar to form a syrup and brush the cooked, hot buns with it.

DECORATED EASTER EGGS

This is an activity for all the family, and although children may prefer chocolate eggs, the excitement of dyeing the eggs and revealing the patterns will have them involved and entertained. If you have your own chickens, slip some of these eggs into their nests on Easter morning and send children to collect them – they will be sure you have magical hens.

hard-boiled eggs
candle, crayon or piece of beeswax
dyes (food colouring, turmeric,
  spinach, onion skins and
  beetroot (beet))

1 Draw any kind of pattern you want on the hard-boiled eggs using a candle, crayon or piece of beeswax.

2 Boil the eggs for a further 5 minutes in the dye of your choice.

3 Pat the eggs dry with kitchen paper.

Left: A basket of coloured eggs make an attractive decoration on Easter day.

Right: Children will love dyeing and decorating eggs.

Halloween

The foods and decorations of Halloween are supposed to echo the occasion, with the decorations being scary and the food bringing comfort. Pumpkins are the main attraction as they are transformed into glowing lanterns and their flesh is made into soups, pies and fritters. Leave children to cut faces in their pumpkins and line them up on the windowsills while you cut star patterns in your pumpkin using pastry cutters to make a table decoration.

PUMPKIN PIE

Many years ago a Danish friend gave me her recipe for a pumpkin pie.

Serves 8
450g/1lb pumpkin
175g/6oz/¾ cup soft light brown sugar
175ml/6fl oz/¾ cup milk
4 eggs
250ml/8fl oz/1 cup double
  (heavy) cream
50ml/2fl oz/¼ cup brandy
10ml/2 tsp ground cinnamon
2.5ml/½ tsp ground ginger or
  grated nutmeg
2.5ml/½ tsp salt
25cm/10in flan tin (pan) lined with
  shortcrust pastry, chilled

Above: *Pumpkin pie.*

1 *Chop the pumpkin into small cubes.*

2 *Steam the cubed pumpkin until soft, about 10–15 minutes, and leave to drain, preferably overnight.*

3 *Preheat the oven to 180°C/350°F/ Gas 4. Place the cooled, drained pumpkin in a food processor with all the remaining ingredients and blend to a smooth texture. Pour the mixture into the prepared pastry case and bake for 1¼ hours.*

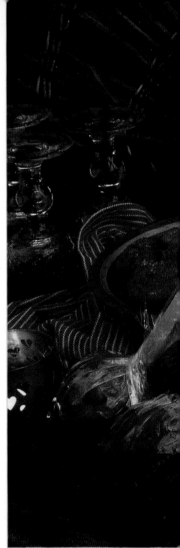

Above: *Colourful pumpkins and squashes.*

PUMPKIN FRITTERS

These moist and delicious fritters
should be eaten while still hot,
sprinkled with cinnamon sugar.

Makes 16–20
75g/3oz/½ cup sultanas (golden raisins)
brandy (optional)
450g/1lb pumpkin, cooked and
* drained*
50g/2oz/½ cup plain (all-purpose)
* flour, sifted twice*

15ml/1 tbsp demerara (raw) sugar
2.5ml/½ tsp baking powder
a pinch of salt
rind of 1 lemon
oil, for frying

Soak the sultanas in a small bowl
of warm water or brandy for about
15 minutes, then drain well. Place the
pumpkin, flour, sugar, baking powder,
salt and lemon rind in a food processor
and blend until the mixture is smooth.

Above: *The Halloween feast – a laden
table lit by glowing candles and spooky
pumpkin lanterns.*

Stir in the sultanas, mixing lightly to
incorporate air into the batter. Heat
the oil in a frying pan and carefully
drop walnut-sized balls of the mixture
into the oil. Cook briefly, turning
once, until the fritters are lightly
browned and float to the surface.
Remove with a slotted spoon.

133

Harvest and Thanksgiving

In the New World, Thanksgiving has superceded the traditional Harvest Festival, which is still celebrated in Europe. Many of the trappings and symbols of the two festivals are very similar. Central to both celebrations is the giving of thanks for the safe gathering in of the harvest.

A DECORATIVE WHEATSHEAF

In pagan times, a miniature stook of wheat in the home would have been an offering to the gods; now it is an attractive country decoration. Traditionally, the farmer's family would make a corn dolly, a braided decoration, from the last sheaf of wheat to be gathered in and this would be brought indoors for the harvest supper and kept in the farm-house until the next harvest.

Above: *A flat-backed container of wheat.*

Many of the corn dollies were extremely elaborate and each family had its own designs. This wheatsheaf is not difficult to make but requires a little patience to achieve a good result. It is made using bunches of wheat bought from a dried flower supplier.

4 bunches wheat
silver birch twigs
string

Undo one bunch of wheat and adjust the heads so that they are level with one another. Once you are satisfied with what you have done, tie the bunch together firmly halfway down the stems. Repeat with two more of the bunches then tie the three completed bunches into one large bunch. Use the remaining bunch of wheat as the outer layer of the wheat-sheaf and tie it in place. Trim the base of the stems level so that the sheaf will stand upright. Twist the silver birch twigs into and around the wheatsheaf and tie them in place.

HEART OF WHEAT

Fashion a wheat heart at harvest time, when the crop is plentiful, for a delightful decoration that would look good adorning a wall or a dresser at any time of the year. Despite its delicate feathery appearance, this wheat heart is quite robust and should last many years.

scissors
heavy-gauge garden wire, or similar
florist's tape
florist's wire
large bundle of wheat ears

Above: *Heart of wheat.*

Cut three long lengths of heavy-gauge wire and bend them into a heart shape. Twist the ends together at the bottom. Bind the wire heart shape with florist's tape. Using florist's wire, make enough small bundles of wheat ears to cover the wire heart shape densely. Leave a short length of wire at each end for fixing to the heart shape. Starting at the bottom, tape the first bundle of wheat ears to the heart. Place the second bundle farther up the heart shape behind the first, and tape it in position. Alternate the angle of the bundle of wheat as you work. Continue until the whole heart is covered. For the bottom, wire together about six bunches of wheat ears, twist the wires together and wire them to the heart, finishing off with florist's tape to neaten.

Right: *A sculptural wheatsheaf bound with silver birch twigs.*

THE HARVEST LOAF

The harvest loaf is traditionally displayed at the altar among the fruit and vegetables and other offerings from the people of the parish. In the past there used to be fierce rivalry between neighbouring parishes as they tried to outdo one another with the intricacy and skill of their designs. Although there were many different designs of harvest loaf, the most enduringly popular was the wheatsheaf, symbolic as it is of the harvest and the vital importance of bread as 'the staff of life'.

Above: *The harvest loaf is in two parts joined by the braided binding.*

Makes two 750g/1¾lb loaves

1.5kg/3½lb/14 cups strong white
* bread flour*
30ml/2 tbsp salt
15g/½oz dried yeast
sugar, to activate the yeast
egg, beaten, to glaze

Sift the flour and salt together into a bowl and make a well. Mix the yeast with 105ml/7 tbsp warm water and a little sugar and leave to activate for 15 minutes. Add the yeast mixture and 750ml/1¼ pints/3 cups water to the flour and mix thoroughly using your hands. Turn out the dough on to a floured surface and knead until the dough becomes elastic. Place the dough in a lightly oiled bowl, cover and leave to prove for 1–2 hours, until it has doubled in size. Preheat the oven to 220°C/425°F/Gas 7. Knock back (punch down) the dough and form the loaf. The high salt content in the dough makes it easier to work, but it is not very palatable.

TO FORM THE LOAF

1 *Take about 225g/8oz of the dough and roll it into a 30cm/12in long cylinder. Place it on a large oiled and floured baking sheet and flatten it slightly with your hand. This will form the long body of the bread, and will be decorated with narrow ropes of dough symbolizing the long stalks of the wheatsheaf.*

2 *Take 350g/12oz of the remaining dough, roll and shape it into a crescent. Place this at the top of the cylinder and flatten. Divide the remaining dough in half. Take one half and divide it in two again. Use one half to make the stalks of the wheat by rolling into narrow ropes and placing on the 'stalk' of the sheaf. Use the other half to make a plait (braid) to decorate the finished loaf where the stalks meet the ears of wheat.*

3 *Use the remaining dough to make the ears of wheat. Roll it into small sausage shapes and snip each a few times with scissors to give the effect of the separate ears. Place these on the crescent shape, fanning out from the base until the wheatsheaf is complete. Position the plait between the stalks and the ears of wheat. Brush the wheatsheaf with the beaten egg. Bake for 20 minutes, then reduce the heat to 160°C/325°F/Gas 3 and bake for a further 20 minutes.*

Right: *The harvest loaf.*

HERBED CORNBREAD

Cornbread is a delicious, moist, cake-like bread that is served at Thanksgiving in recognition of the importance of the maize harvest to the American people. This herbed cornbread, made with herbs of your choice, is a delicious variation that deserves to be eaten more than once a year.

Makes 16 x 5cm/2in squares

165g/5½oz/generous 1¼ cups plain (all-purpose) flour
125g/4½oz/generous 1 cup yellow cornmeal
65g/2½oz/generous ¼ cup sugar
15ml/1 tbsp baking powder
3.75ml/¾ tsp salt
250ml/8fl oz/1 cup milk
1 large (US extra large) egg
30ml/2 tbsp unsalted butter, melted and cooled
30ml/2 tbsp finely chopped fresh herbs of your choice (chives, rosemary and oregano are especially delicious)

Preheat the oven to 220°C/425°F/Gas 7. Sift the dry ingredients together into a bowl. In another bowl, beat the milk, egg, butter and herbs. Stir the liquid ingredients into the dry ones until just combined. Pour into a buttered 20cm/8in square tin (pan). Bake for 15 minutes until puffed and golden. Using a skewer, check that the centre is cooked. Cut into squares and serve warm with butter.

CRANBERRY, SULTANA AND WALNUT TART

This is an ideal dessert for anyone who is not madly keen on cranberries but feels that they are an essential part of the celebration.

Serves 6–8

225g/8oz/1⅓ cups fresh cranberries
250g/9oz/scant 2 cups sultanas (golden raisins)
115g/4oz chopped walnuts
115g/4oz/½ cup demerara (raw) sugar
50ml/2fl oz/¼ cup maple syrup
15ml/1 tbsp brandy
grated rind of 1 orange
25cm/10in flan tin (pan) lined with shortcrust pastry, chilled
25g/1oz/2 tbsp cold unsalted butter, cubed

Preheat the oven to 220°C/425°F/Gas 7 and preheat a baking sheet. Combine the cranberries and sultanas in a bowl. Add all the remaining ingredients, except the butter, and toss so that the cranberries, nuts and sultanas are coated. Pour into the pastry case and dot the surface with the butter. Place on the preheated baking sheet and bake for about 15 minutes, then reduce the heat to 180°C/350°F/Gas 4 and bake for 30 minutes.

CRANBERRY AND ORANGE SAUCE

Cranberries are from the New World and this sauce, which accompanies the Thanksgiving turkey, has also

Above: *Orange zest is one of the flavourings in the cranberry, sultana and walnut tart.*

become an essential part of Christmas dinner in many parts of the world.

Makes 500g/1lb 2oz

225g/8oz cranberries
175ml/6fl oz/¾ cup fresh orange juice
115g/4oz sugar
30ml/2 tbsp Grand Marnier
5ml/1 tsp grated orange rind

Cook the cranberries in the orange juice until they are soft; this should take about 5 minutes. Remove from the heat and add the remaining ingredients. Finally, spoon the sauce into clean, dry jars and cover. Keep the sauce in the refrigerator until used.

It is vitally important to make sure that you do not overcook this sauce, because the cranberries will develop a rather unpleasant bitter taste.

Right: *The pantry's shelves are groaning with delicious Thanksgiving food.*

Above: *Squares of herbed cornbread.*

Christmas

Most of us are nostalgic for the traditional country Christmas, even if we have lived all our lives in the city; each year we optimistically think this year's festivities will be the perfect Christmas – and just occasionally it is. A laden table will appear with no dramas in the kitchen or harassed cooks, the tree will look magical, relatives will all love one another and the children will be filled with rosy-cheeked wonder. One of the secrets of an enjoyable Christmas is not to try to do it all. The event should be a celebration for everyone, even the organizer, and a few things done well will give more pleasure than tired and resentful hosts.

A CHRISTMAS GARLAND

A colourful, welcoming garland on the door sets the scene for Christmas. The natural materials create a wonderful texture and wired ribbon will be able to stand up to all but the most extreme of weather conditions. The coarse sisal rope bows make an interesting contrast to the luxurious bows.

florist's wire
30cm/12in straw ring
carpet moss
German pins
blue pine
12 x 30cm/12in cinnamon sticks
6 large cones
3m/3¼yd x 7.5cm/3in wide ribbon
9 poppy seedheads
sisal string

1 *Use a length of wire to attach a small loop to the straw ring to allow you to hang the garland. Cover the ring with carpet moss, pinning it in place with the German pins.*

3 Wire the cinnamon sticks into three bundles and, using the German pins, attach them to the garland. Attach wires to the base of the cones by twisting them around the scales of the cones and pin them on to the garland close to the cinnamon sticks.

Cut the ribbon into three pieces and fold each into a double bow using wire to secure the bows. Pin the bows to the garland over the cinnamon sticks and cones. Tuck the poppy seedheads into the folds of the bows and pin them in place. Tie three bows using the sisal string, fray the ends and then pin them on to the garland.

Above: *Cones and seedheads for the Christmas garland.*

2 *Cut the blue pine into short lengths and pin them on to the garland.*

Right: *Soft blues and greens give this pretty Christmas garland a Scandinavian look.*

MULLED WINE

In days past when people rode on horses or took drafty carriages to their neighbours' houses at Christmas, mulled wine was a necessary restorative to the circulation. Today, most of us can travel in warmer and more comfortable conditions, but the taste and aroma of this spiced drink is an established part of Christmas.

Serves 10

2 bottles smooth red wine
2.5ml/½ tsp whole allspice berries
1 cinnamon stick
6 cloves
115g/4oz/½ cup sugar
6 drops Angostura bitters
rind of ½ orange

Place all the ingredients in a pan and heat gently without boiling until the sugar has dissolved.

EGGNOG

This spectacular Christmas drink is for some unknown reason far more popular in America than in Britain, but it makes a delicious and warming festive drink and deserves to be enjoyed all over the world.

Serves 6

6 large (US extra large) eggs,
* separated, at room temperature*
200g/7oz/1 cup caster
* (superfine) sugar*
300ml/½ pint/1¼ cups brandy
50ml/2fl oz/¼ cup dark rum
500ml/17fl oz/2¼ cups milk
120ml/4fl oz/½ cup double
* (heavy) cream*
15ml/1 tbsp vanilla extract
salt
freshly grated nutmeg

Using an electric mixer, beat the egg yolks until pale. Gradually mix in the sugar until the mixture thickens. Whisk in the brandy, rum, milk, cream and vanilla. In a separate bowl

Above: The heat of the mulled wine releases the fragrance of the cinnamon.

whisk the egg whites with a pinch of salt until they make soft peaks. Fold the whites into the yolk mixture and decant into a serving bowl. Chill for 3 hours. Before serving, stir the eggnog gently and sprinkle with freshly grated nutmeg.

BUTTERED RUM

A delicious alternative to mulled wine, this drink will warm the cockles of your heart.

Serves 6

4 cinnamon sticks
20ml/4 tsp soft light brown sugar
120ml/4fl oz/½ cup dark rum
600ml/1 pint/2½ cups dry cider
25g/1oz/2 tbsp unsalted butter
rind of ½ lemon
2.5ml/½ tsp ground mace

Warm four tisane glasses or mugs. Place a cinnamon stick, a teaspoon of sugar and a quarter of the rum in each glass. Gently heat the cider without boiling and pour it into the glasses. Top with butter, a curl of lemon rind and a sprinkling of mace.

GLÖGG

Glögg is an extremely potent and dramatically pyrotechnical drink which is great fun to serve at Christmas parties. It should be prepared and drunk with caution as you will discover from the instructions below.

Serves 6–8

4 whole allspice berries
muslin (cheesecloth)
4 cardamom pods
1 cinnamon stick
10 ready-to-eat dried
* apricots, halved*
2 bottles dry red wine
225g/8oz sugar cubes
600ml/1 pint/2½ cups aquavit or
* vodka, warmed*
300ml/½ pint/1¼ cups cognac,
* warmed*
nuts, unsalted
raisins

Tie the spices in a piece of muslin, place in a pan with the apricots and wine and heat. When the wine begins to simmer, remove the bag of spices and pour into a warmed heatproof bowl. Place a wire cake-rack over the bowl. Build a pyramid of the sugar cubes on the rack, making sure the construction is solid.

Gently pour on the warmed aquavit or vodka, ignite at arm's length, then pour on the cognac. Or, ignite the aquavit or vodka in its pan and gently ladle it over the sugar. The sugar will melt as it burns and fall through the rack into the bowl.

When the flames have died down, pour the drink into heatproof glasses or mugs, to which a few raisins and nuts have been added. Make sure that each person gets half an apricot.

Right: The rich colours of Christmas are enhanced by the glasses of mulled wine, which have been filled to welcome the guests.

FRESH DATE CAKE

Make this wonderful fat-free cake each year as a delicious, yet light alternative to the usual rich Christmas cake; the perfect antidote, to be eaten with a cup of lightly fragrant tea at the point when you never want to see another mince pie ever again.

Makes a 1kg/2¼lb cake
350g/12oz/2½ cups fresh dates
125g/4½oz/generous ½ cup glacé
(candied) cherries
125g/4½oz/generous 1 cup self-raising
(self-rising) flour
125g/4½oz/¾ cup caster
(superfine) sugar
2.5ml/½ tsp salt
225g/8oz coarsely chopped brazil nuts
25g/1oz shredded fresh coconut
1 large (US extra large) egg
30ml/2 tbsp brandy

Above: *Stuffed dates.*

Preheat the oven to 150°C/300°F/ Gas 2. Remove the skins from the dates, cut them in half and remove the stones (pits). Wash the cherries to remove the syrup and then quarter them. Sieve the flour, sugar and salt together into a large mixing bowl. Add the fruit, nuts and coconut and then toss so that every single ingredient is well coated with flour. Whisk the egg with the brandy, add it to the bowl and mix thoroughly.

Pour the mixture into a greased and lined 1kg/2¼lb loaf tin (pan) and bake for 1¼ hours.

KUMQUATS AND LIMEQUATS IN BRANDY SYRUP

These yellow and green fruits are highly decorative as well as tasting very good indeed. Make a few extra jars to give to friends and family as presents, and why not spoil yourself and open a jar for a treat and eat a few of the fruits spooned over some vanilla ice cream as a quick-and-easy pre-Christmas dessert.

Makes 500g/1lb 2oz, plus syrup
450g/1lb kumquats and limequats
175g/6oz/scant 1 cup sugar
150ml/¼ pint/⅔ cup brandy
15ml/1 tbsp orange flower water

Using a cocktail stick (toothpick), prick each individual fruit in several places. Dissolve the sugar in 300ml/ ½ pint/1¼ cups water over a gentle heat then bring to the boil. Add the fruit and simmer for about 25 minutes until it is tender. Drain the fruit and spoon into hot, sterilized jars. The syrup should be fairly thick; if it is not, boil it for a few minutes, then allow it to cool only very slightly. Add the brandy and the orange flower water to the syrup. Pour the syrup over the fruit and seal immediately. Store in a cool place and use within six months.

Above: *Kumquats and limequats in brandy syrup.*

STUFFED DATES

Slivers of crystallized ginger give a bite to these fresh dates stuffed with marzipan and topped with halved walnuts. They are delicious served with coffee. Packed into a decorative box, they make an unusual and thoughtful gift.

24 fresh dates
50g/2oz crystallized ginger
115g/4oz marzipan
24 walnut halves

Using a sharp knife, slit the dates along their length and then carefully remove the stones (pits). Chop the ginger into fine slivers and work them into the marzipan. Place a walnut-sized piece of marzipan in the cavity of each date and top with a halved walnut. The dates must be stored in the refrigerator and used within a week.

Right: *Home-made edible gifts are always much appreciated at Christmas.*

Seasonal Checklist

Evocative descriptions and timely reminders of tasks
to be done throughout the year.

Spring

Spring is the season of new growth – of aromatic mint, broad-leaved sorrel and tender spikes of chives picked in their infancy to garnish young salad leaves or to pack in among baby vegetables freshly lifted from the garden and bottled for enjoying during the winter months. It is a time for flavoured butters drizzled over grilled (broiled) vegetables and fish, of scented oils and vinegars and delicate flower cordials. It is the season of youth; all is green and yellow and there is a crisp, fresh fragrance in the air. It is a time of renewal when we spring clean homes as unveiled windows reveal dusty corners, and we gently nourish our tender, winter-dried skin before we bare it to the warming sun.

IN THE GARDEN:
- Clean out the greenhouse and cold frame, washing down the windows and removing an disposing of any dead or diseased plants.
- Sow flower, vegetable and herb seeds, making fortnightly sowings of salad crops.
- Cut early herbs for use in salads and for making flavoured oils and vinegars.
- Dig up early potatoes.

IN THE PANTRY:
- The pantry should be looking quite bare right now and this is a good opportunity to wipe down shelves and throw out anything that is past its best. It may be an idea to make a note of what you needed more of and what was less popular.
- Collect all the empty jars and bottles together, check that they have lids and replace rubber rings and seals where necessary.
- Bottle choice baby vegetables with new season herbs.
- Make flavoured oils, vinegars and mustards.

IN THE BATHROOM:
- Use the body scrub and washing grains to invigorate and cleanse the skin after winter.
- Make new batches of lotions, tonics and hair rinses.

IN THE STILL ROOM:
- Dry flower petals and herbs for future use in potpourris and scented sachets.
- Make a new batch of beeswax polish and furniture reviver ready for spring cleaning.
- Throw out any dried flowers and herbs that are looking tired and dusty and replace with fresh flowers picked from the garden.

SEASONAL CELEBRATION:
- Make a simnel cake at least two weeks before Easter Sunday so that is has time to mature.

Left: Bring a breath of spring into your home with an arrangement of daffodils, tulips and hyacinths, freshly cut from the garden.

Above: *An orchard (if you happen to have one!) is the perfect place to plant great banks of daffodils, but don't mow the area until they have died right down or every year they will produce fewer and fewer flowers each spring.*

Right: *The delightful little crocus is one of the earliest and most cheerful of spring flowers, and even the least knowledgeable of windowsill gardeners should find space for a pot of these pretty flowers.*

Summer

As the sun climbs higher in the sky the greater heat it gives out intensifies taste and fragrance. The delicate flavours of spring give way to robust ripeness as tomatoes turn a deep luscious red and we marry their marvellous flavour with peppery basil and the fruitiest of olive oils. Strong flavours and colours are the order of the day: herbed mustards and marinades for barbecues; refreshing teas to be drunk in the shade; vibrant flowers and herbs, gathered in the morning when their fragrance is at its most intense for using fresh or for drying.

IN THE GARDEN:
- After the last frosts, move plants outside from the greenhouse and cold frame.
- Harvest herbs and flowers for drying.
- Dig up main crop potatoes and harvest onions, garlic and shallots as they are ready.

IN THE PANTRY:
- Throw out the remnants of last year's dried herbs and replace with newly dried herbs.
- Bottle fruit and vegetables when they are in their prime.
- Make jams, jellies and curds from soft fruit.
- Blend herbal teas.

IN THE BATHROOM:
- Make herbal infusions and use in lotions, tonics and creams.
- Dry some herbs for use in later infusions.

Above: *The pleasure of being able to gather your own flowers from the garden is one of the joys of summer.*

IN THE STILL ROOM:
- Dry flowers for potpourris and arrangements.
- Make lavender bags and other scented sachets or dry the ingredients for use later.
- Make insect-repellent candles for use in the garden and near open windows.

SEASONAL CELEBRATION:
- Make sure you find time to enjoy summer in the garden.

Left: *Sun-ripened tomatoes, freshly picked from the garden, have an intensity of colour and flavour that makes them irresistible and far superior to those found in superfmarkets.*

Left: *Summer yields a bounty of fresh garden salads that can be picked minutes before serving to enthusiastic diners at your al fresco dinner party.*

Below: *A warm wall in the garden is an ideal place for a fan-trained peach or apricot tree and can yield a surprisingly good harvest of fruit.*

Autumn

Left: *Choose the variety of apple tree you grow with great care; it will be with you a long time and eating the fruit should be a pleasure not a chore.*

Below: *Autumn is the best time to go hunting for sweet chestnuts in woods and meadows. Always check with an expert before eating.*

As the hedgerows stoop under the weight of ripening berries and the trees drop their leaves, the golden light of autumn burnishes all it touches. In woodlands, scurrying creatures gather food in preparation for the coming months and the air is rich with the scent of ripeness and decay. This is the time of year when the urge to preserve and store is at its strongest, when every country walk is an opportunity to gather, when even the most urbanized of us may make a pot of jam or jelly, taking pleasure in such a simple task. Children, however far removed from the land, pause to appreciate nature and the farmer at Harvest Festival or Thanksgiving.

IN THE GARDEN:
- Pick fruit from the orchard and vegetables from the kitchen garden and store and preserve for winter.
- Bring tender plants into the greenhouse and cold frame before the first frosts.
- Pot up herbs for the kitchen windowsill.
- Gather seeds for drying ready to sow next year.

IN THE PANTRY:
- Make jams, jellies, pickles and chutneys.
- Prepare herb and spice mixes.
- Bottle fruit and vegetables.

IN THE BATHROOM:
- Make nourishing creams and lotions for face and body.
- Check through your essential oils and replace any that are too old or running low.
- Make up new batches of massage oils and lotions to revive tired muscles after clearing the garden.

IN THE STILL ROOM:
- Make beeswax candles.
- Make up new dried flower arrangements and batches of potpourri to decorate and fragrance the home over the coming year.

SEASONAL CELEBRATION:
- Make up a basket of produce for the Harvest Festival.
- Bake a harvest loaf.
- Make pumpkin lanterns and pumpkin pie for Halloween.

Right: *With their marvellous shapes and vibrant colours, squashes and gourds are wonderfully ornamental as well as full of flavour.*

Winter

Winter at its best is a bright crisp day with frost or snow underfoot, but all too often it is a procession of dreary grey days of unrelieved gloom, which can depress the most optimistic among us. This is the time of year when we can take pleasure in our earlier labours and feast on the flavours of spring and summer that are filling the shelves of our store cupboard or pantry. It is a time to nurture ourselves with delicious foods, to luxuriate in scented baths and to pamper ourselves with tempting sweetmeats. It is the season of giving, when we can make gifts for our friends and family and fill our homes with the smells of traditional spices that are an essential part of the Christmas festivities. It is a time to look forward, and in doing so, we complete the cycle and once again greet the coming of spring.

Above: *Those main crop vegetables that were stored in autumn now come into their own as they are used in warming soups and stews.*

IN THE GARDEN:
- Scrub pots and seed trays ready for seed sowing in the spring.
- Read the seed catalogues – and dream.
- Gather Christmas greenery early and stand in water in an outhouse or garage.

IN THE PANTRY:
- Enjoy using the fruits of your labours.
- Make sloe gin.
- Check the spice cupboard and replenish any stocks that are low.
- Use Seville oranges to make marmalade.
- Dry Seville orange skins for cooking and potpourris.
- Candy citrus peel.
- Make food presents ahead of the Christmas preparations.

IN THE BATHROOM:
- Make new batches of bath oils for winter dry skin.
- Prepare a new batch of rich hand cream and healing ointment to treat winter-ravaged skin.

IN THE STILL ROOM:
- Make bird treats to hang in the garden.

SEASONAL CELEBRATION:
- Make the Christmas garland at least two weeks before the festivities.

Top: *Dried beans and pulses are a useful standby . . .*
Above: *. . . although still no match for fresh winter vegetables.*

Above: *A well-stocked bird table will help many of the garden and woodland birds, not to mention the odd squirrel, survive through the harshest of winters, as well as providing you with hours of enchanting entertainment. Make sure you position it somewhere where cats cannot jump on to it.*

Right: *Between the vegetable garden and the cold frame you should be able to pick vegetables and herbs all winter.*

Useful sources and suppliers

UK
Suppliers of essential oils

Aromantic Ltd
17, Tytler Street
Forres
Moray
IV36 1EL
Tel: 01309 696900
http://www.aromantic.co.uk

Hermitage Oils
20 Clifford Avenue
Kingston Upon Hull
HU8 0LU
Tel: 01482 711432
http://www.hermitageoils.com

Neal's Yard Remedies
Many stores nationwide and
worldwide, as well as online and by
mail order
Tel: 0845 262 3145
http://www.nealsyardremedies.com

**Suppliers of medicinal and
culinary herbs**

Potters Herbal Supplies
1 Botanic Court
Martland Park
Wigan
WN5 0JZ
Tel: 01202 449752
http://www.pottersherbals.co.uk

Hambleden Herbs
Rushall Organic Farm
Devizes Road
Rushall
Wiltshire
SN9 6ET
Tel: 01980 630 721
http://www.hambledenherbs.com

**Suppliers of natural
beauty ingredients**

G Baldwin & Co
171–173 Walworth Road
London
SE17 1RW
Tel: 020 7703 5550
www.baldwins.co.uk

**Suppliers of dried flowers and
potpourri ingredients**

The Hop Shop
Redmans Lane
Sevenoaks
Kent TN14 7UB
Tel: 01959 523219
www.hopshop.co.uk

Robson Watley International
Crocodile House
Heathfield
TN21 9LQ
Tel: 01424 838564

Suppliers of cut herbs and plants

Iden Croft Herbs
Frittenden Road
Kent TN12 0DH
Tel: 01580 891432
http://www.uk-herbs.com

USA
Suppliers of essential oils

The Body Shop
Online and numerous stores
nationwide and worldwide
http://www.thebodyshop-usa.com

Kiehl's
Online and numerous stores
nationwide and worldwide
http://www.kiehls.com

LorAnn Oils
4518 Aurelius Road
Lansing
Michigan 48909
Tel: (517) 882-0215
https://www.lorannoils.com

**Suppliers of medicinal and
culinary herbs**

Caprilands Herb Farm
534 Silver Street
North Coventry CT 06238
Tel: (860) 742-7244
http://www.caprilands.com

Richter's Herb Catalog
357 Highway 47
Goodwood
ON
L0C 1A0 Canada
Tel: +1.905.640.6677
http://www.richters.com

Suppliers of dried flowers and potpourri ingredients

Dried Flowers Direct
from Keuka Flower Farm
3597 Skyline Dr., Penn Yan
NY 14527
(315) 694-9021
www.DriedFlowersDirect.com

Gail Ann's Floral Catalog
821 W. Atlantic Street
Branson, MO 65616

Nature's Finest
P O Box 10311, Dept. CSS
Burke, VA 22009

Val's Naturals
P O Box 832
Kathleen, FL 33849
http://www.valnatural.com

AUSTRALIA
Suppliers of essential oils

Australian Botanical Products (abp)
Tel: (03) 9709 4800
http://www.abp.com.au

Bridestowe Estate Pty Ltd
296 Gillespies Rd
Nabowla
Tasmania Australia 7260
Tel: (03) 6352 8182
http://bridestowelavender.com.au

Suppliers of medicinal and culinary herbs

Herbs of Gold Pty
P.O Box 3143
Kirrawee NSW 2232
Tel: 1800 852 222
www.herbsofgold.com.au

Southern Light Herbs
P O Box 227
Maldon
Vic. 3463
Tel: (03) 5475 2763
http://www.southernlightherbs.com.au

Suppliers of dried flowers and potpourri ingredients

Yuulong Lavender Estate
Yendon Rd
Mt Egerton
Vic 3352
Tel: (03) 5368 9453
http://www.yuulonglavender.com.au

Hedgerow Flowers
32a Glynburn Rd.
Hectorville 5073
Tel: +61 8 8336 1623
http://www.hedgerowflowers.com.au

Index

A
Almond oil cleanser, 92
Anchovy butter, 41
Apples: apple cake, 68
  Kashmir chutney, 36
  rosehip and apple jelly, 50
  storage, 25
Apricots: dried apricot jam, 52
Artichokes in olive oil, 39
Autumn (fall), 152, 153
  potpourri, 103

B
Bain-marie, 14
Beetroot (beet): pickled beetroot, 60
  thinnings, 16
Berries, gathering, 16
Bird nut ball, 122
Borax, 83, 84, 90
Bottles: labelling, 31
  preserving, for, 30
  seals, 31
  sterilizing, 28, 29
Bread, 70, 71
  bread pudding, 70
  Harvest loaf, 136
Butters, flavoured, 40, 41

C
Cabbage: pickled red, 60
Cakes, 68
Calendula cream, 110
Candied peel ribbons, 56
Candles, 114
Carnauba (carnahuba), 77, 90
Cayenne salt, 44
Celery salt, 44
Chamomile and peppermint
  tisane, 67
Cherries in eau de vie, 58
Chilli oil, 32
Chocolate and walnut
  fudge, 72
Christmas, 140–4
Chutneys, 36
Coconut ice, 72
Cold cream, 90
Containers, 30
Cosmetics, making, 76, 77
Courgette (zucchini)
  teabread, 68
Crab apple jelly, 50
Cranberry and orange
  sauce, 138
Cranberry, sultana and walnut
  tart, 138
Creams and lotions, making, 77

D
Damson jam, 52
Dates: fresh date cake, 144
  stuffed dates, 144
Dill pickles, 38
Door sachets, 104
Dried flowers: basket of, 120
  buying, 27
Drying, 28
Dusting powders, scented,
  88

E
Easter, 128–30
Easter eggs, 130
Eggnog, 142
Elderberry syrup, 62

Elderflower cordial, 62
  tea, 110
Essential oils, 15, 80, 81
  mixing, 82

F
Festivals, 126, 127
Flowers: drying, 26, 27
  flower oils, 81
  health and beauty, for, 78
Folk tales, 12
Frankincense, 81, 114
Fruit: boiled fruit
  cake, 68
  bottled fruit in syrup, 58
  candied, 56
  fresh, 14
  fruit oils, 80
  gathering, 16
  growing, 16
  harvesting, 17
  preserved, 58, 59
  quality, 24
  storage, 24
  tasting, 24
Fruity tree, 122
Furniture reviver, 112

G
Garlands, 116–18
 Christmas, 140
Garlic, 110
 garlic butter, 41
 garlic oil, 32
Geranium oil, 83
Ginger: candied, 56
 ginger honey, 55
 rhubarb and ginger jam, 54
Glögg, 142

H
Hair rinses, 96
Halloween, 132, 133
Hand creams, 94
Harvest and Thanksgiving, 134–8
Healing ointment, 94
Heart of wheat, 134
Herbal bath bags, 84
Herbal infusion, 76
Herbed cornbread, 138
Herbs: displaying, 18
 drying, 26
 growing, 14, 26
 harvesting, 17, 26, 27
 health and beauty, for, 78
 herb butters, 40
 herb oils, 80
 plaited (braided) herb loaf, 71
 salt, preserving in, 26
Honey: flavoured, 55
 honey mustard, 48
Horseradish, mustard, 48
 traditional horseradish
  sauce, 42
Hot cross buns, 130

I
Ingredients, 14, 15

J
Jack's pickled shallots, 39
Jams (jellies): damson jam, 52
 dried apricot jam, 52
 making, 13
 pots, decorating, 20
 rhubarb and ginger jam, 54
 setting point, testing, 50
 labelling, 31
 preserving, for, 30
 seals, 31
 sterilizing, 30
Jellies: crab apple jelly, 50

 rhubarb and mint jelly, 52
 rosehip and apple jelly, 50
 setting point, testing, 50

K
Kashmir chutney, 36
Kumquats and limequats in brandy
 syrup, 144

L
Lanolin, 84, 90, 94
Lavender: bags, 106
 body lotion, 84
 bubble bath, 84
Lemons: lemon and lime curd, 54
 lemon and lime vinegar, 34
 lemon mix, 46
 lemon pepper, 44
 orange and lemon tea, 66
Limes: lemon and lime curd, 54
 lemon and lime vinegar, 34
 lime butter, 40
Luxurious body scrub, 86

M
Malt bread, 70
Marigold
 cream, 110
 flower oil, 81, 82, 110
 and verbena tisane, 66
Marmalade, orange, 52
Massage oil, 82
Materials, 14
Medicines, 110

Mint: caution, 78
 chamomile and peppermint
  tisane, 67
 mint sauce, 42
 peppermint body lotion, 84
 peppermint sachets, 108
 rhubarb and mint jelly, 52
Moisture creams, 90
Moth repellent sachets, 108
Mulberry ratafia, 64
Mustards, flavoured, 48

N
Nuts, gathering, 16

O
Oil treatment for hair, 97
Oils, flavoured, 32, 33
Orangeflower water, 78
Oranges: orange and grapefruit bath
  oil, 86
 orange and lemon tea, 66
 orange and oatmeal washing
  grains, 92
 orange marmalade, 52
Organically grown foods, 16
Origanum, 78
Orris, 102, 104, 106, 108

P
Packaging, 20
Patchouli oil, 80, 94, 102
Peaches: brandied peaches, 58
 peach wine, 64

Pears: pickled pears, 38
  spiced pears, 59
  windfall pear chutney, 36
Pepper: flavoured, 44
  mixed peppercorns, 44
Pickles, 36–9
Polishes, 112
Pomanders, 104
Potpourri, 102, 103
Pregnancy, 76, 84, 102
Preserves: labelling, 31
  making, 13
Preserving, 28
  containers, 30
Pumpkin: pumpkin fritters, 132
  pumpkin pie, 132

Q
Quatre epices, 46

R
Raspberry vinegar, 34
Ratafia, mulberry, 64
Remedies, 110
Rhubarb: rhubarb and ginger jam, 54
  rhubarb and mint jelly, 52
Roasted pepper butter, 40
Room fresheners, 104
Rose-lavender-scented cushion, 108
Rose petal tea, 66
Rose-scented sachets, 108
Rosehips: rosehip and apple jelly, 50
  rosehip syrup, 62
Rosemary vinegar, 34
Rosewater, 78
Rum, buttered, 142

S
Saffron oil, 32
Salt, 10
  flavoured, 44
Simnel cake, 128
Skin tonics, 92
Sloes: gathering, 16
  sloe gin, 64
Spice islands potpourri, 102
Spices, 46, 100

Spring, 148, 149
Sterilizing: bottles, 28, 29
  jars, 30
Still room, history of, 100
Store cupboard (pantry): basics, 14
  history of, 10
  using and displaying, 18
Summer, 150, 151
  potpourri, 102
Swags, 116–18

T
Tarragon: tarragon and Champagne
    mustard, 48
  tarragon vinegar, 34
Teas, 66
Tea tree massage lotion, 80, 83, 94, 96
Teriyaki marinade, 33
Tisanes, 66
Tomatoes: bottled cherry tomatoes, 60
  green tomato chutney, 36
  storage, 24
  tomato ketchup, 42
Truffles, 73

V
Vanilla honey, 55
Vegetables: bottled, 60, 61
  fresh, 14, 15
  growing, 16
  harvesting, 17
  quality, 24
  storage, 24, 25
  tasting, 24
  vegetables in olive
    oil, 39
Vinegars: cleaning, 113
  flavoured, 34

W
Wheatsheaf, 134
Whisky honey, 55
Witch hazel, 110
Wholemeal (whole-wheat) loaf, 70
Wild flowers, 16
Wine: mulled, 142
  peach wine, 64
Winter, 154, 155
Wood oils, 81

ACKNOWLEDGEMENTS

Thanks to:
Holly McIntntyre for her valued assistance with preparing projects and searching out props.
Liz Trigg for her help with the food projects.
Michelle for her inspired photography and good company.